"If your loved one has a problem with compulsive saving, this book can help you both save what really counts—yourselves! With equal parts compassion, wisdom, and practicality, Michael Tompkins and Tamara Hartl offer step-by-step instructions for helping family members and friends with hoarding challenges. The authors' passion for their work comes through on every page, and their extensive experience is evident in every nugget of advice they offer."

—Jeff Bell, author of *When in Doubt, Make Belief: An OCD-Inspired Approach to Living with Uncertainty*

"An essential guide for loved ones of those who compulsively hoard. *Digging Out* takes a compassionate approach to both the hoarder and the family member's perspective and offers practical tools that really work to reduce harm associated with clutter and improve family relationships."

—Belinda Lyons, executive director of the Mental Health Association of San Francisco

"*Digging Out* is a remarkable book. Michael Tompkins and Tamara Hartl walk the reader step-by-step through the difficult process of letting go of unrealistic expectations, healing old wounds, and helping loved ones get much-needed help for compulsive hoarding. This book is likely to become a must-read for family members of people with significant hoarding problems."

—David F. Tolin, Ph.D., ABPP, director of the anxiety disorders center at The Institute of Living and adjunct associate professor of psychiatry at Yale University School of Medicine mental health professionals. It provides a clear method, harm reduction, that has been proven effective in reducing the dangerous consequences of hoarding, yet also promotes positive relationships between the hoarder and his or her loved ones. The authors are to be commended for the benefits offered by *Digging Out* to the many people who have to cope with this disabling disorder."

—Paul R. Munford, Ph.D., clinical psychologist and director of the Cognitive Behavioral Therapy Center for OCD and Anxiety in San Rafael, CA

"*Digging Out* is a wonderful book for those who have family members or other loved ones with compulsive hoarding and cluttering problems. It provides a practical, realistic, in-depth, and empathic approach to helping manage this serious and often debilitating problem using harm-reduction techniques. This book manages that most difficult of combinations—providing hope and guidance without minimizing potential obstacles to success."

—Carol A. Mathews, MD, associate professor of psychiatry at the University of California, San Francisco School of Medicine

"Undoubtedly, *Digging Out* is one of the best available texts for assisting the families of those suffering from hoarding and cluttering to declutter and help their loved ones live in a healthy environment. I highly recommend the book for all who work with or may come across people struggling with hoarding and cluttering."

—Johnson Ojo, REHS, special programs manager, San Francisco Department of Public Health

Digging Out

HELPING
YOUR
LOVED ONE
MANAGE
CLUTTER,
HOARDING &
COMPULSIVE
ACQUIRING

Michael A. Tompkins, Ph.D.
Tamara L. Hartl, Ph.D.

New Harbinger Publications, Inc.

Publisher's Note

This publication is designed to provide accurate and authoritative information in regard to the subject matter covered. It is sold with the understanding that the publisher is not engaged in rendering psychological, financial, legal, or other professional services. If expert assistance or counseling is needed, the services of a competent professional should be sought.

NEW HARBINGER PUBLICATIONS is a registered trademark of New Harbinger Publications, Inc.

Distributed in Canada by Raincoast Books

Copyright © 2009 by Michael A. Tompkins & Tamara L. Hartl
New Harbinger Publications, Inc.
5674 Shattuck Avenue
Oakland, CA 94609
www.newharbinger.com

All Rights Reserved

Acquired by Tesilya Hanauer; Cover design by Amy Shoup;
Edited by Nelda Street; Text design by Tracy Marie Carlson

Library of Congress Cataloging-in-Publication Data on file

Printed in the United States of America

24   23   22

15 14 13 12 11 10

To Luann, Madeleine, and Olivia, who make the trip worthwhile.

—Michael A. Tompkins

To the memory of my grandfather, Linwood Wotton, whose wisdom continues to influence which challenges I choose to accept.

—Tamara L. Hartl

Foreword

Until a few short years ago, hoarding was virtually unknown to the mental health community. Even now, many mental health treatment providers do not know how to treat hoarding, although it is quite likely that some of their clients have had hoarding problems that they did not divulge. In contrast, hoarding has been all too real to family members of people who struggle with their possessions. Every year we receive hundreds of pleas from desperate and frustrated family members who are worried about the health and safety of their hoarding loved ones. Their fears are well founded. Hoarding is a serious condition that threatens the health, the safety, and even the lives of people who suffer from it. Home conditions of someone with a serious hoarding problem can also threaten the health and safety of family members and neighbors, not to mention others, such as firefighters, who must enter and exit such dwellings in an emergency. Hoarding also carries the risk of eviction.

Hoarding has an enormous impact on relationships as well. Many people who hoard have great difficulty establishing and maintaining a marriage. They are less likely to marry and more likely to divorce (Kim, Steketee, and Frost 2001). The primary culprit in these undeveloped and fractured relationships is the cluttered condition of the home and the fact that normal living—eating, sleeping, bathing, and socializing—becomes too difficult. When the excessive acquiring and clutter pushes out the partner, and the person who hoards ends up alone, the level of clutter often escalates, putting the person at even greater risk.

Family members who call us are mostly the sons and daughters of a middle-aged or older parent who has developed a serious hoarding problem. The callers are frustrated and angry, but at the same time worried about their parent's future. Most have made numerous attempts to help. These efforts follow a common storyline.

First, family members offer to assist in cleaning and discarding. Before long, tension develops as the son or daughter tries to discard something of value to the parent. The adult child sees little value in the item and tries to convince the parent to get rid of it. The parent becomes focused on stopping such interference. A battle of wills ensues, with little chance of success on either side. Frustrated and sometimes angry, family members often attempt to remove items without the knowledge of their loved one. Discovery provokes an angry exchange and a refusal to allow the son or daughter back into the house—or sometimes into the parent's life. At this point family members may give up and declare their parent incorrigible or call the authorities to investigate. The upshot is strained relationships, or worse yet, complete estrangement.

These well-meaning attempts fail because the hoarding loved one and the concerned family member have vastly different perspectives about possessions, neither able to acknowledge or understand the other's views. To the family member, the problem is clutter, and as soon as it is cleared out, their loved one will be safe and happy. To the hoarding loved one, the problem is control over cherished possessions, which will be secure only when the family member stops trying to make decisions about these belongings.

It is a pleasure to herald *Digging Out*, a much needed volume for anyone who has struggled with family members about hoarding. Michael A. Tompkins and Tamara L. Hartl have created a protocol that offers hope for family members who have long felt hopeless. They give direction and purpose to those struggling with and frustrated by a family member who can't control his or her attachment to things. The tasks laid out in this book are not easy. In fact, following these wise recommendations may be the hardest thing family members have ever done. But the approach described in this book will produce a deeper understanding of the hoarding syndrome and potentially a relationship beneficial to both the person who hoards and the family member. Tompkins and Hartl's harm reduction approach provides a way to repair family relationships and use them to effectively manage the most troublesome parts of the hoarding problem. It is a must-read for people who care about their family member who hoards.

—Randy O. Frost, Ph.D.
Harold and Elsa Siipola Israel Professor of Psychology
Smith College

—Gail Steketee, Ph.D.
Professor and Dean
Boston University School of Social Work

Acknowledgments

This book wouldn't have been possible without the seminal work of a number of researchers who've dedicated their professional lives to understanding the problem of compulsive hoarding and to developing ways to help those who suffer with it. Although this is a long list, we want to thank, in particular, Randy O. Frost, Gail Steketee, and David F. Tolin for their generous and consistent support of our ideas.

We thank Belinda Lyons, executive director of the Mental Health Association of San Francisco (MHA-SF), for her enthusiastic support of our book. In addition, we acknowledge MHA-SF and its key role in disseminating information about compulsive hoarding. We thank the members of the San Francisco Task Force on Compulsive Hoarding, under the aegis of the San Francisco Department of Aging and Adult Services, MHA-SF, and other professionals, for their support of this project. These professionals include Gary Hartz, Thomas L. Hafemeister, Joe Cuff, Martha Legallet, Joel Liberson, Jason Wolford, Cindy E. Rasmussen, Aregawie Yosef, and Monika Eckfield. We also thank Alan and Linda Merrifield of Peninsula Community Services for maintaining an informative website devoted to providing resources for people who hoard and their families.

We thank our editor, Tesilya Hanauer, for her enthusiastic support of this book and for her tolerance of our many missteps along the way. We thank Jess Beebe, senior editor at New Harbinger, for improving the quality of the book in general.

I, Michael, thank my colleagues at the San Francisco Bay Area Center for Cognitive Therapy, beginning with Jacqueline B. Persons, director, who continues to encourage me to try things that seem to me to be just beyond my reach. I thank my other colleagues at the center (Joan Davidson, Janie Hong, Katherine Martinez, and Daniel Weiner) for their continued support of my professional development. I would also like to thank my wife, Luann L. DeVoss, and my daughters, Madeleine and Olivia, for tolerating yet another book project. They are troopers and I love them dearly.

I, Tam, thank my colleagues at the VA Palo Alto Health Care System (Judith Chapman, Bob Hall, and Jeanette Hsu) for their ongoing support, and Jim Moses for being the first person to order the book before we even completed it. I also thank Randy O. Frost, George J. Allen, and Toni Zeiss for their invaluable mentorship along the way. I thank my husband, Stuart, for giving me the time and space for writing, his earnest interest in the work itself, and his ingenious idea of a reward system that included Indian food when I completed milestones in the writing project. He truly embodies the meaning of "life partner" and makes me feel lucky every day. Finally, I thank my mother, Beverly, and my sister, Kristin, for being wonderful role models, for their love and support, and for rooting for me in this and all endeavors.

Finally, we acknowledge those who've taught us the most about the problem of compulsive hoarding: those who suffer with the problem and the family members and friends who love them. They have enriched our lives through their trust and inspired us by their courage and determination to better their situations. We have altered the descriptions of clients, family members, professionals, and our work with them to protect their privacy.

Introduction

Gloria and Kathy are desperate. Their mother is seventy-eight years old and lives in the family home surrounded by tons of paper, books, and all manner of debris. She has scabies and respiratory problems from living in her trash-filled home, and several weeks ago, she stumbled over the clutter and broke her wrist. Yet she refuses to let her daughters clear and clean her home. Gloria and Kathy have argued and reasoned with her, cajoled and threatened her. They've offered to move her into a lovely retirement home and invited her to live with either of them, but she still refuses any help at all. Now, after years of arguing with her and sneaking trash out the back door, they're no longer allowed into her home.

Jim has given up. He's bitter about the years his father appeared to care more about his stuff than about him. He remembers years of shame and embarrassment about his littered home and the way kids called him "pigsty" and made "oink" sounds when he walked by them at school. He remembers days without power, heat, or running water because his father had either lost the bill or wouldn't let anyone into the house to repair the damaged toilet, sink, or furnace. Jim is angry that he has had to lie about his father's problem for years. As a kid, Jim lied to his friends about why they couldn't come to his house for sleepovers. As an adult, he lies to his children about why they never go to their grandpa's house, and he lies to his father's neighbors when they call him to complain about the debris in his father's yard. Now, even if his father wanted help, Jim isn't sure he could put all the bitterness aside and reach out to him.

About one to three million people in the United States (Samuels et al. 2008) have a hoarding problem, a typically lifelong pattern of acquiring and keeping almost everything. But a great many others, like Gloria, Kathy, and Jim, suffer as well. Spouses, adult children, aunts, uncles, and friends live in terror that their loved one will perish in a fire or beneath an avalanche of refuse and trash. They're ashamed that their loved one lives in a littered home infested with rodents and roaches, or without heat or a working toilet. They're bitter and angry because they've lived for years with the problem and with their loved one's refusal to accept help from them or anyone else. In many cases, the problem has damaged formerly loving and caring relationships. Over time, families grow hopeless because they don't see a realistic way to solve the problem, in part, because what they've tried hasn't worked, or at least hasn't worked well.

For Those Who Are Open to Help: Treatments That Work

This book is for family members of people who both hoard and have little or no insight about the problem and therefore have refused treatment or help. However, if you're one of the lucky few with a loved one who's open to treatment, we urge you to help her find it. Two treatments appear to help some people with compulsive hoarding: cognitive behavioral therapy and medications for other problems that can make it more difficult for your loved one to work on his hoarding problem.

Cognitive Behavioral Therapy for Hoarding

Cognitive behavioral therapy (CBT) for hoarding includes a series of strategies to help your loved one learn to control her urges to acquire and save, to sort and organize her possessions, and to let go of possessions a few at a time. Typically, the therapist goes to the person's home periodically to show him how to apply what he learned in the office therapy sessions. Recent research shows that CBT helps the majority of people who hoard to declutter and feel better (Tolin, Frost, and Steketee 2007a). However, few people are actually "cured" at the end of eight months of CBT, because the people who complete CBT still have more clutter than the average person does when treatment ends. In addition, we don't know how well people can control their hoarding problems after treatment ends.

Some mental health professionals, such as psychologists, psychiatrists, and social workers, provide CBT. However, because CBT is a specialized form of psychotherapy, we recommend that you verify whether the mental health professional is an expert in CBT and whether he or she has experience in treating compulsive hoarding. The appendix at the end of this book provides information for finding professionals who are knowledgeable in CBT for compulsive hoarding. In addition, if your loved one is interested in CBT, we recommend *Buried in Treasures: Help for Compulsive Acquiring, Saving, and Hoarding* (Tolin, Frost, and Steketee 2007b), a landmark text on the psychological treatment of compulsive hoarding, or *Overcoming Compulsive Hoarding: Why You Save and How You Can Stop* (Neziroglu, Bubrick, and Yaryura-Tobias 2004).

Medications

Many people who hoard take medications used to treat obsessive-compulsive disorder (OCD). These include serotonin reuptake inhibitors (SRIs) such as clomipramine, and selective serotonin reuptake inhibitors (SSRIs) such as fluvoxamine, fluoxetine, sertraline, and paroxetine. However, it's not clear how useful these medications really are for treating hoarding, but if your loved one is open to a trial of medications, we urge you to arrange an evaluation with someone with expertise in prescribing these medicines. Although medications may not greatly improve your loved one's hoarding problem, they can still play an important role in a comprehensive plan for helping your loved one *manage* her hoarding problem. For example, many people who hoard have other conditions, such as depression, inattention, or health problems, that can make it more difficult for them to work on the hoarding problem even in small ways. Depression, for example, can decrease your loved one's motivation to organize his possessions or declutter a room, as well as diminish his ability to concentrate or tolerate the distress when he does. Similarly, inattention, as in the case of someone with attention-deficit disorder (ADD), can interfere with your loved one's ability to focus and stay on task when organizing or sorting possessions. Medications may be helpful for these problems.

In spite of the promise of treatments such as CBT, most clinicians and researchers agree that hoarding is extremely difficult to treat. In addition, it appears that only a minority of those who suffer with this problem actually seek treatment. Therefore, family members, not the person who hoards, more often seek help and search for resources and information on the topic.

We've written this book primarily for you: the family members of people who hoard. In this book, we describe *harm reduction*, which is an approach that recognizes that many people who hoard have little or no insight about their hoarding problem and therefore don't seek help or treatment for the problem, even when living in the most squalid of conditions. Harm reduction is a pragmatic alternative to treatment for compulsive hoarding when the person who hoards has refused treatment outright, when the treatment is floundering, or when family members or other caregivers have simply run out of time and ideas.

Why They Refuse Help

If your loved one suffers from compulsive hoarding, you've likely tried to help. You may have offered to clean her home or to hire someone to do it. You may have suggested that your loved one meet with a therapist or talk about the problem with a doctor; you may have purchased books on the topic and given them to your loved one to read, or searched for hours on the Internet for resources that could help—and, to all these efforts, your loved one has said no. Your loved one's refusal to accept help, or even to admit that there's a problem, is perhaps the most frustrating and demoralizing aspect of the problem for family members.

Although some with the problem do see that the clutter is excessive and that their living conditions are unsafe and uncomfortable, they may be in the minority. Far more people who hoard tend to resist or avoid treatment or help. They appear baffled by family members' reactions to the clutter and are oblivious to the risks and discomfort that come from living with too many things. Typically, these people are older and have suffered from the problem of compulsive hoarding for years, often decades, and live in very dilapidated and unsafe conditions. They tend to minimize the severity of the situation with comments such as, "My house isn't that messy," and show little awareness of the problem, even though they may be smart and rational in other ways. Typically, when these people do accept help, it's because others have forced it upon them. Even when refusing help may mean eviction, some people still say no.

Poor insight, disagreement about how to solve the problem, fear, hopelessness, resentment and mistrust, and personal values are some of the reasons your loved one refuses help.

Poor Insight

We describe people who don't appear to recognize that their thoughts or behaviors are excessive or irrational as having poor or low insight. The adult daughter of a woman who had hoarded for thirty years described her mother in this way, "My mother's a very bright woman—she's a Phi Beta Kappa, for god's sake—but when it comes to her stuff, it's as if she has a hole in her brain. She just doesn't get it." Compulsive hoarding certainly appears to be a condition of low insight, as are other psychiatric conditions, such as psychotic disorders (particularly schizophrenia), bipolar disorder, and OCD. Because low insight prevents people who hoard from perceiving that they have a problem, they don't believe they need help. However, this isn't to say that people who hoard never feel distressed or uncomfortable. Many do. Most often, however, they're distressed only when other people either prevent them from saving more things or when community public health officials force them to clear out their possessions or face eviction.

The simple fact of the matter is this: people don't see that there's a problem unless they feel distressed by it. That's why you're more eager to solve the hoarding problem than your loved one: the hoarding problem bothers you more than it does your loved one, and no amount of reasoning, cajoling, arguing, or threatening is likely to change that.

Disagreement About the Best Solution

Sometimes people who hoard admit that they have a problem but don't see it the same way family members do. Your loved one may tell you that it's not that bad or that it really doesn't interfere with his life all that much, and certainly he'll scoff at the idea of seeking help or treatment for the problem. Instead, your loved one will suggest that you help him find more space to store his acquisitions or to remove a few things from his home when what he needs is a much larger clear-out intervention.

Janice had an interesting take on her mother's situation. She accepted that she and her mother had different solutions to the hoarding problem: "I wanted my mom to wake up and smell the coffee. I wanted her to let me help her clear out her home so that she could sleep on her bed, eat at her kitchen table, and use her stove and refrigerator. The bottom line for me was that I wanted my mom to get rid of the stuff so that she could live more comfortably in her home. My mom saw it very differently. She wanted to figure out a way to live more comfortably in her home with her stuff. That meant figuring out a way to make more room in her life for more stuff rather than clear out her stuff to make more room for her life."

Disagreement about the best solution to the hoarding problem often leads to endless and circular discussions about what to do. At first, both the family members and the person who hoards believe that they're working on the problem. Only later, after many arguments and hard feelings, do they realize that they're digging in rather than digging out.

Fear

Often people who hoard refuse help because they're afraid. They may fear discovery and eviction or that others will come into their homes and, in a frenzy of helping, clear out all of their possessions. Due to fear of discovery, they often live in squalid conditions, because they don't permit people into their homes who could repair the refrigerator, stove, or leaky toilet. If they rent, they never complain to the landlord about a broken pipe or furnace, because they fear the landlord will want to come into the apartment to have a look around. They know at some level that if others discover the hoarding problem, they'll suggest, perhaps insist, that something be done. This fear isn't unreasonable, because if the problem is discovered, that discovery may lead authorities to remove all or most of the possessions or to even evict your loved one from his home.

If you have a family member who hoards, you may fear discovery of the problem as well. If the landlord evicts your loved one, where will he go? You may not be able to afford alternative housing for your loved one, such as a retirement or assisted-living facility. Even if you can afford alternative housing for your loved one, you may be worried that the facility's managers won't accept her if they know that she has a hoarding problem. If an assisted-care facility refuses your loved one, would you want him to live with you, knowing that the hoarding problem would accompany him? For these reasons, at times family members help their loved ones keep the secret, not just because they themselves are ashamed about the problem but also because they know that once the problem is discovered, their lives and that of their loved one will be in the hands of strangers. George spoke of this dilemma:

> *I could tell that my mom was scared that someone would find out about her hoarding problem. At first, I thought that would be great. Let someone discover the problem and force her to clean up her act. I figured that people would come in and clear out the stuff, and then she could live a few more years in her house and be a little more*

comfortable. However, over the years, as the problem worsened, I realized that if other people discovered the problem, they might force her out of her home permanently. I didn't want that for her—or for me! I'm ashamed to say it, but I don't want my mom living with me and my family, not because I don't love her but because I just can't live with her stuff anymore, and I can't afford to pay for a retirement home for her either. So I stopped telling her to get help and started to help keep her secret.

Hopelessness

Many people who hoard refuse help because they don't believe they can really change. This is particularly true for people with severe hoarding problems who've acquired and saved for thirty or forty years or more. The idea of clearing a home filled with decades of possessions is indeed daunting. The task likely would take many days, if not weeks, of effort by many people. People who hoard tell you that they've tried to solve the hoarding problem. They remember working many hours each day organizing, moving, or going through their possessions with the goal of clearing their homes, yet their homes largely remained the same. They feel hopeless that any real change can happen, and they give up. Other people who hoard accept help clearing out their possessions but soon find that the problem creeps back. As they grow older, it becomes harder and harder to try again, and they become more and more hopeless that any real and sustained change is possible.

Resentment and Mistrust

Another reason why people who hoard refuse help is that they no longer believe that they can ask others, such as family members, for support, in part because everyone involved in the hoarding problem feels bitter, resentful, and angry. Hoarding problems dissolve formerly caring and compassionate relationships into bitter and volatile ones. Most family members of people who hoard remember years of arguing, yelling, and screaming about what to keep and what to throw away. They're bitter and resentful about missing out on birthdays or holidays because they couldn't invite anyone to their homes. Or, even when a holiday was celebrated among the piles of paper and refuse, these family get-togethers soon soured at the first mention of Mom's or Dad's hoarding problem.

Adding to this emotional burden is the effect of eroded trust and goodwill. Most people who hoard tell stories of family members coming into their homes and carting boxes away without permission. They tell us how a daughter invited them out for breakfast, while a son cleared a room of stuff. They're hurt and angry as they ask us, "Whom can I trust now? Whom could I ask for help if I even wanted it?" On the other side, family members tell us that they had no choice but to remove their loved one's possessions because they could no longer sleep at night out of fear for the safety of their mother or father. Some family members tell us that given the choice, they would do it again—if they could get back into the house. Others tell us that they're deeply ashamed of their deceptive behavior but had tried everything else and nothing had worked.

For example, Bob's father refuses to speak to him now, but Bob remembers many good years when he was young. His father, who is now eighty-eight years old, once played professional baseball, and Bob was proud of that and the great baseball memorabilia his father owned. Over the years, however, Bob watched in horror as his father began to collect everything. They began to argue repeatedly about what to keep and what to discard until Bob grew more and more angry and resentful. One day he took matters into his own hands:

> *I'm not proud to say this, but after awhile, I just started sneaking things out the back door. When my father was away, I would come over and take out stacks of newspapers from the garage or a cardboard box or two from under the bed. I figured my father would never miss the stuff, but I was wrong. One day he confronted me and called me a thief. He said I was stealing from him, and I called him crazy and stormed out. After that, he never let me into his home again. At first, we would speak on the phone, but after a while that stopped. He said all we ever did was argue. He was right. The only thing we seemed to talk about was his stuff. And you know what, he was right about another thing. This is tough for me to admit, but I did steal from him. It was his stuff, and I took it. I walked into my father's home and stole from him.*

Personal Values

Often people who hoard refuse help because their acquiring and saving, as well as the possessions themselves, confer on them a special and valued role or sense of importance. In other words, hoarding satisfies a set of important values for the person who hoards. This is why it's so very difficult to give up hoarding behaviors. Even if a person who hoards has insight into the problematic nature of the hoarding, certain deeply held values related to possessions can make it very difficult for her to change. Although people who hoard may very much value their relationships to family members and desperately want to repair the damage that the hoarding problem has caused, they simultaneously value the meaning their possessions confer on them. Your father may see himself as the man with all the answers and thereby justify his acquiring and saving as a way to have, when you need it, the name or telephone number of a family member or friend, the list of summer camps for your children, or an interesting television or radio program that he has recorded. Similarly, your mother may believe that her possessions represent a personal virtue. She may see herself as a woman with great aesthetic sensibilities and therefore keep all manner of interesting magazines, postcards, and fabric swatches.

Mollie, for example, saw herself as someone who took great care to find the perfect gift for each of her twelve nieces and nephews, perfectly matched to each child's interests and tastes. Her family saw this as a virtue too, telling Mollie that she was the perfect aunt who always knew just the right thing that would please even the most particular niece or nephew. Mollie began her holiday shopping in the summer and spent several months wrapping each gift in exquisite wrapping paper. However, to find the perfect gift, she had to buy many of them, and to wrap the gift in the perfect way, she had to have an endless number of choices of wrapping paper and ribbon. Although Mollie's family appreciated her thoughtfulness, they were concerned at the amount of wrapping paper, ribbons, and unopened gifts that cluttered her home. For people who hoard, possessions become the means to satisfy personal values, which is true for many of us. The difficulty is not the values of the person who hoards but the manner in which he sets about satisfying those values, which, in the extreme, can become both inefficient and dangerous.

Digging Out

If you're reading this book, you haven't given up hope for your loved one, although you may wonder whether it's worth trying again. As the spouse, adult child, brother, sister, parent, or friend of a person who hoards, you likely have suffered and still suffer under the enormous weight of your loved one's countless possessions.

However, another weight may trouble you: the heavier emotional weight of years of hurt, fear, resentment, shame, and loss. You may feel bitter and angry because your loved one has repeatedly refused to accept help for the hoarding problem. You may have awakened many a night worried that your loved one has set a stack of newspapers on fire or that the head-high pile of trash has tumbled and buried her. You may feel ashamed that your loved one lives in a littered home infested with rodents and roaches, or lacking heat or a working toilet. You may be heartbroken that you can't take your children to visit their grandmother. You may feel devastated because, even when you threatened your partner with divorce, he chose his possessions over you.

If you grew up in the home of a person who hoards, you may resent the damage done to your life and the lives of your brothers and sisters. You know that your childhood was not the same as those of other children. You never had friends visit or sleep over at your house. You had to make endless excuses to friends and family members for why they couldn't visit. You still remember the way other children taunted and rejected you because of the condition of your home. Even if you can help your loved one dig out from under the piles of debris and possessions, you may wonder whether you can ever dig out from under the weight of the damage years of relentless acquiring and saving have done to the relationship between you and your loved one.

In this book, we hope to help you and your loved one dig out from under the weight of both burdens: the countless possessions and the damaged relationships. Digging out takes time, but if you're patient and realistic, you can do it. Many of the ideas we present here will seem odd. However, they rest on two important assumptions: First, people change when we help them set realistic goals. Second, people change when we give them valid and meaningful reasons to work toward those goals. We've discovered that people who hoard agree to accept help not because they necessarily want to live in a clean and orderly environment free of so many possessions. They accept help because they want to reconnect with friends and family, celebrate holidays and occasions in their homes, or have their grandchildren visit them; or they do it because they want their family members to find some value in their possessions rather than forever urge them to throw out things. Thus, the harm reduction approach outlined in this book assumes that people will change if others work with them to set realistic goals and give them valid and meaningful reasons to work toward them. This principle is the backbone of our approach and supports everything that follows.

How to Use This Book

Our aim in writing this book is to provide you, the family member of a person who hoards, with an approach that can help you manage your loved one's hoarding problem, either alone or in collaboration with other caregivers and professionals. The goal is pragmatic: to manage the hoarding problem over time so that your loved one can live safely and comfortably at home.

If you've just begun to believe that your loved one may have a hoarding problem, we recommend beginning with chapter 1, "What Is Compulsive Hoarding?" to familiarize yourself with the nature of compulsive hoarding and to learn whether your loved one has this problem. In chapter 2, "Harm Reduction," we describe our approach to the problem of compulsive hoarding and explain how this approach might help you and your loved one manage the problem.

In chapter 3, "Setting the Stage for Harm Reduction," and chapter 4, "Helping Them Accept Help," we describe how to begin the task of helping your loved one accept help, how to set the stage for the harm reduction approach, and how to introduce a new way of working together. We recommend reading both chapters 3 and 4 before discussing the harm reduction approach with your loved one. He'll likely have many questions about the goals of harm reduction, particularly because it's likely, at various points, to include the removal of possessions. In addition, these chapters speak to the complicated feelings you have about your loved one who hoards. Although you desperately want to help, we recognize the great price you've paid over the years for loving someone with a hoarding problem.

In chapter 5, "Assessing Harm Potential," chapter 6, "Creating a Harm Reduction Plan," and chapter 7, "Keeping the Harm Reduction Targets Clear," we describe how to go about putting together a harm reduction team, creating a harm reduction plan, and working with your loved one over time to keep her home safe and comfortable. Chapter 8, "Managing the Bumps in the Road," describes strategies for managing the inevitable ups and downs of keeping a harm reduction plan going over many months and years. In addition, we present guidelines for using appropriate pressure when the hoarding situation is public and authorities are threatening to evict your loved one from his home or apartment.

Chapters 9 and 10, "All in the Family and Other Complications" and "When the Landlord Knocks, and Other Terrors," provide information on other topics of interest to family members of people who hoard. They describe the particular challenges of assisting old and frail family members who hoard, helping those who live in assisted-care or shared-housing facilities or who live with other people who hoard (such as a spouse, parent, or child). This section of the book takes up topics such as if and when to consider a guardianship or conservatorship for your loved one, what to do when child or adult protective services become involved with the hoarding problem, or when and how to stage a clear-out intervention. Finally, the appendix includes information on professionals and organizations that can assist family members in creating and maintaining a harm reduction plan.

Although you may believe that your loved one is beyond help, take heart. We've seen this approach work when the goals were clear and realistic, and when all those involved in the harm reduction approach were dedicated to the same goal: helping the person who hoards live safely and comfortably at home. At this moment, even that goal may seem unreachable, but with patience and the right approach, we believe you can make it happen.

CHAPTER 1

What Is Compulsive Hoarding?

We all have stuff: a kitchen drawer filled with old thumbtacks, rusty door hinges, or spools of thread that we keep "just in case." Over the years, if we aren't thoughtful about what we keep and what we discard, our garages, closets, and drawers fill with more and more stuff. We tell ourselves we'll get around to clearing it out someday, but we never do. Yes, we all have stuff. But when does our stuff become a problem—a problem for us and for the people who love us?

In this chapter, we define compulsive hoarding to help you better understand what it is and what it's not. We present four problem areas at the core of compulsive hoarding that we hope will explain why your loved one appears to cling desperately to her possessions and why the problem has worsened over the years. If you're uncertain whether your loved one has the problem, we'll present some signs to look for. We then present other conditions that may exist along with hoarding behavior.

Defining Compulsive Hoarding

Norman is eighty-eight years "young," as he likes to joke, and few people would disagree with that assessment. He has the energy and interests of a twenty-eight-year-old. He tells anyone who'll listen about his years in Paris as a struggling art student and about his lifelong love of everything beautiful. Norman once owned a large graphic design company, but now that he's retired, he fills his days by collecting art—and anything else that his lively and creative eye catches. He has filled his home with postcards advertising gallery exhibits that opened forty years ago, interesting photos and pictures clipped from magazines and newspapers over the years, scraps of colorful cloth, buttons with a "special sparkle," and even old cereal boxes with interesting pictures on the front. His son and daughters have grown more and more alarmed with his collecting, particularly because it appears to have worsened since his wife died. They've suggested that he give some things to them or that he donate some of his cherished collection to a local art school, but he seems overwhelmed by the idea of getting rid of anything, even the smallest postcard. Does this sound like your family member? If so, your loved one might be suffering from *compulsive hoarding*.

Compulsive hoarding appears to be a common problem. Researchers estimate that the problem occurs in about four to five out of every thousand individuals throughout their lifetimes (Samuels et al. 2008). The prevalence of hoarding symptoms among people with dementia may be substantially higher (Hwang et al. 1998). Because hoarding symptoms accompany a wide range of mental health conditions, and because, in many cases, the sufferer hides the condition out of fear of discovery, the true prevalence of hoarding may be much higher than current estimates suggest.

There are four factors central to compulsive hoarding: excessive acquiring, difficulty discarding, living in cluttered spaces, and having significant distress or impairment. Let us look at these distinct features of the problem.

Excessive Acquiring

People who hoard typically cannot stop acquiring. They bring objects home even if they don't need them, or even if they already own one or more of them. They purchase items intending to give them as gifts, but they seldom do. They shop at garage sales, sort through Dumpsters, and bring all manner of interesting items to already overfilled homes. Many people who hoard compulsively make purchases from their favorite websites and bid for items in online auctions. They often continue to purchase when they've run out of money or available storage space, and they do so in the face of threats from bill collectors and family members. People who hoard also tend to bring home free things and extras whenever possible: brochures, newspapers, and extra handouts from seminars or talks. They fill their closets and drawers with "just in case" items, for example, bag after bag of plastic stir sticks and packets of salt, pepper, and sugar.

Difficulty Discarding

Most people who hoard keep the same things as everyone else (newspapers, junk mail, old receipts, notes or lists, magazines, bags, books, boxes, and clothing). Once people who hoard bring something into their homes, however, it becomes almost impossible to get it out again. Family members are often dismayed when their loved one refuses to discard items that appear useless or unnecessary, such as a shoe without a mate or clothing they've outgrown. Dismay, however, can turn to disgust as family members watch their loved one keep items that others would describe as waste, such as half a doughnut or carrot stick, nail clippings, used disposable bandages, or excrement.

Many people who hoard don't get rid of things because they want to avoid making a decision about whether to keep something or let it go (Frost and Gross 1993). Keeping the item by default becomes the way out of this dilemma. At times, the person who hoards does discard a possession, but doubts about the decision begin to creep in and she soon retrieves the item from the trash. Other people who hoard experience a sense of grief or profound loss when they discard possessions and soon learn that by avoiding discarding anything, they avoid reexperiencing intense feelings of grief and loss.

Living in Cluttered Spaces

Another central component of compulsive hoarding is cluttered living spaces. A person who hoards may not be able to get to his bed because of the piles of clutter. Papers, books, and bags cover the chairs, sofa, and dining table so that they can't be used to rest, watch television, or eat a meal. Cluttered floor spaces make it difficult to move freely from room to room. In addition to living spaces, clutter may extend into other areas, such as the car, yard, garage, work environment, storage units, or storage areas that belong to family members or friends.

Having Significant Distress or Impairment

People who hoard often feel embarrassed; avoid inviting others into the home; can't find things; and often argue with spouses, family members, or both about their possessions and the hoarding problem. Many people who hoard are extremely socially isolated. They may not have had visitors to the home for several years. Many people who hoard can't cook meals, do laundry, or use their showers or toilets because these spaces are filled with clutter or because their appliances are broken and they're afraid to let someone into the home to fix them.

Hoarding also causes problems at work. Employers sometimes fire people who hoard because of their hoarding behaviors. In some cases, people who hoard face eviction or the removal of children or elders from the home. Thus, hoarding profoundly impairs the day-to-day functioning of people with a hoarding problem.

Some people who hoard refer to themselves as "collectors," and by that, they mean that they see themselves as people who collect rather than hoard. There has been little research into what reliably differentiates hoarding from collecting. However, since we're discussing impairment here, this is often where hoarding and collecting part ways. In general, collectors don't have to step over their collections in their homes and can still use their beds and appliances. That is, they've organized their collections, carefully cataloged them, or displayed them in a way that doesn't interfere with day-to-day activities. Some people who hoard may refer to themselves as collectors or some other term that feels less pejorative to them. Regardless of what you or your loved one calls it, if it's getting in the way of safety or relationships, it has likely metamorphosed from a hobby into a problem.

Hoarding also has a profound impact on family members of those who hoard. You may fret because much of your loved one's money goes to purchasing this and that or to paying to store her possessions. The relationship with your loved one may be sour and difficult, which adds to the stress of just trying to keep your loved one out of harm's way. Family members also have to contend with angry protests from landlords who threaten to evict their loved one, or face the possibility that authorities might remove a child or elder from the home because it's too dangerous for people to live there. As a result, family members of people who hoard feel helpless, frustrated, and hopeless about the hoarding problem and its effect on them and their loved one.

Despite the far-reaching consequences that hoarding has on a person's life, people who hoard may not recognize the problems that hoarding behaviors cause. Similarly, not all people who hoard experience distress from the hoarding behaviors. In fact, it may be incomprehensible to you that your loved one doesn't seem bothered by the condition of his home, especially when you, significant others, neighbors, or health and safety personnel are extremely distressed about the situation.

Why Save *That*?

The reasons why people who hoard save possessions aren't unlike the reasons why most people save things. For example, people who hoard save possessions for sentimental reasons or out of an aesthetic appreciation for the form, color, beauty, or other aspect of the possession. In addition, people who hoard save possessions because they intend to use them someday. They view possessions as having a useful function and value each because they intend to use the item someday, even if they've never used the item before. The unlimited number of uses for an item only complicates the person's belief that she might need it someday. People with hoarding behaviors are extremely creative in coming up with countless hypothetical uses for a given possession. For example, people who hoard might keep an empty tin because they see its limitless possibilities. Someday, they might use it as a pencil cup, a small plant holder, a money jar, part of an art project, a cookie cutter, a rolling pin, or a scoop for laundry detergent. Thus, a tin can is not just a tin can in the eyes of the person who hoards. For this reason, simply asking the person whether he has used the item in the past wouldn't make him feel any more comfortable about getting rid of it since the object represents a world of ways to use it somehow.

The Many Potential Uses of an Everyday Object

To get you in touch with the agony of a lost opportunity that your loved one may feel when asked to discard something, try this exercise. On a blank piece of paper, write as many uses as possible for a cap from a plastic water bottle. See if you can think as broadly and creatively as a person who hoards. Having thought of so many uses, do you still want to throw that cap away?

Scoring:

1–5 uses: Good first attempt, but we think you can come up with more if you give it more time. Is "cat toy" on your list, for example?

6–10 uses: Not bad! This is a respectable number of possible uses. However, if you didn't write "cookie cutter," you still have some untapped creativity in you that needs to come out.

11–15 uses: Well done! You're able to think creatively about how to use a bottle cap.

16 or more uses: Outstanding! Your mind sees the limitless possibilities for an everyday object.

Why People Keep Hoarding

Four primary problem areas help explain what makes it difficult for people to stop hoarding: information-processing difficulties, emotional attachments to possessions, unhelpful beliefs about possessions, and avoidance behaviors (Frost and Hartl 1996).

Information-Processing Difficulties

Information-processing difficulties include problems with attention, organization and categorization, and decision making. These difficulties are interrelated and profoundly affect a person's ability to organize possessions and throw things away.

DIFFICULTIES WITH ATTENTION

Problems with attention make it difficult for people who hoard to stay on task when they're trying to organize possessions or decide what to discard. When your loved one tries to organize her possessions, she may be able to work only a few minutes before getting distracted by something she sees in the clutter or before getting up to wander around her apartment. In addition, decluttering can make your loved one very anxious, which can make it even more difficult to work on the hoarding problem for more than a few minutes.

PROBLEMS WITH ORGANIZATION AND CATEGORIZATION

People who hoard have great difficulty categorizing and organizing possessions. They're *underinclusive* in their approach to categorization. For example, if you set about organizing all your sales receipts, you might organize them by the month shown on the sales receipt, which would mean that you would need twelve file folders. However, your loved one might worry that he'll forget into which month he placed the receipt, and therefore he'll want to organize his receipts into more categories (by the month on the sales receipt, by the type of item purchased, and by a budget category). More categories would mean more file folders until your loved one assigns every possession its own unique category such that it would be impossible to organize or group possessions in a meaningful way. Furthermore, when your loved one treats each possession as unique, he increases the value of the possession and thereby transforms the possession into something invaluable and irreplaceable.

People who hoard use very inefficient strategies to deal with clutter, which contributes to the hoarding problem. They sort through their possessions repeatedly, a behavior called *churning* (Frost and Steketee 1999), with an intention to organize and store items, but they end up putting things somewhere "just for now." Through churning, and because they have few clear places to do routine activities, such as paying bills, reading the newspaper, or having a cup of tea, they mix different possessions (overdue bills, canceled checks, tea bags, newspapers) together to create random piles throughout the house. Last, people who hoard organize in a horizontal rather than vertical fashion, in an effort to keep everything in sight. Papers end up stacked on tabletops and counters rather than filed in a file cabinet.

DIFFICULTIES WITH DECISION MAKING

People who hoard have great difficulty making decisions about what to keep or save and where to store a possession and how, as well as making the many other choices required to sort and organize possessions efficiently. Often, the decision-making process overwhelms them and they simply stop trying to organize their possessions. If your loved one can't decide whether to keep something, she'll always opt to keep it. If she can't decide where to store something, she'll always opt to put it back down where it was. If she can't decide whether to start clearing the counter or the sofa, she'll opt to wait until later to begin clearing at all.

Emotional Attachments to Possessions

People who hoard often regard their possessions as extensions of themselves, to the extent that throwing something away can feel as if they've abandoned a dear friend. Familiar objects and possessions comfort and reassure your loved one. They become a "friend" that your loved one values and trusts. In exchange, your loved one assumes the responsibility of caring for the possession. Because of their intense emotional attachment to possessions, people who hoard experience severe distress when others touch, move, or discard their possessions and may feel personally or emotionally violated.

Unhelpful Beliefs About Possessions

The way we think about things typically has an effect on how we behave. Many thoughts and beliefs help to maintain the hoarding problem by making it difficult to discard possessions or move them out of view. These unhelpful beliefs about possessions include beliefs about responsibility, beliefs about the need for perfection or to have something "just right," and beliefs about memory.

BELIEFS ABOUT RESPONSIBILITY

People who hoard believe that they should be responsible by being prepared at all times. This translates into carrying extra "just in case" items and saving possessions so that they'll never be without a needed item. People who hoard also feel responsible for the well-being of the possession itself. Consequently, many people who hoard strive to recycle or donate a possession whenever possible rather than discard it, or find a good home for it with a friend or family member.

BELIEFS ABOUT THE NEED FOR PERFECTION

People who hoard believe that they must find the perfect use or the perfect owner for a possession in order to relinquish it. If they're storing an item, they believe they must devise the perfect way to store it. They believe they must clean or repair a possession to restore it to perfect condition before they can give it away. Similarly, people who hoard may believe that they must complete a task perfectly. For example, they may believe they must read every word in every newspaper or collect every magazine in a series. Not doing so would lead to sensations of imperfection similar to an itch that can't be scratched. The sense that something isn't "just right" can immensely frustrate people who hoard.

BELIEFS ABOUT MEMORY

People who hoard often say that they have the hardest time remembering things. They lack confidence in their ability to remember and tend to exaggerate the importance of remembering things. The lack of confidence in memory shows up in several ways. People who hoard may opt to save written information, in part because they don't trust that they'll remember it without a tangible reminder. In addition, this doubt about their ability to remember information may explain why people who hoard often want to keep possessions in sight rather than in storage spaces. As a result, they clutter their living spaces with items in an effort to keep things in view.

In addition, people who hoard often believe that they should be able to remember what people without a hoarding problem would find difficult to remember. For example, people without hoarding problems probably wouldn't beat themselves up over being unable to remember the entire contents of last Sunday's newspaper. However, people who hoard believe they should remember what was in that paper, and the easiest way for them to do that is to save it. People who hoard are often worried and frustrated by what they perceive to be memory problems, when the real problem is that they've set a standard for remembering that's frustratingly unattainable.

Avoidance Behaviors

People who hoard avoid making decisions about possessions and avoid discarding, which results in an accumulation of possessions and leads to increasingly cluttered living spaces. This, in turn, leads to more clutter, which makes the prospect of organizing, storing, or discarding even more daunting. Saving possessions, rather than discarding them, becomes a way for people who hoard to control how they feel. In choosing to save everything, the person can prevent the possibility of regretting a decision to throw something away.

How Do You Know if Your Loved One Has the Problem?

As you've learned, there are a number of factors that can make it difficult to sort out whether your loved one has a compulsive hoarding problem.

First, hoarding affects people and families in many different ways, so no two cases of hoarding are quite the same. Some people who hoard collect items that you clearly know are trash or garbage. They've littered their homes with food containers, moldy newspapers, or even scraps of food. On the other hand, some people who hoard collect items that you, too, may collect, such as fabric, books, craft supplies, or interesting artifacts. The problem here isn't *what* they collect but how much of it they keep and how cluttered their living spaces are.

Second, many people who hoard insist that they don't have a problem. They admit that they're a bit messier than you are but insist that they have everything under control. They have plans for all their possessions and just need some time to organize and put things away. Third, just as beauty is in the eye of the beholder, so is messiness. We have different comfort levels when it comes to cluttered or messy living situations. It's not always clear when it comes to clutter whether someone has a problem.

Next, we provide a checklist describing some warning signs that may reveal that your loved one has a hoarding problem. Check off any items that you think apply. Remember, these are warning signs. For the reasons we previously gave, your loved one may not actually have a hoarding problem. If you're not certain, though, seek out a mental health professional with experience in evaluating and treating hoarding problems. The professional can evaluate your loved one and help decide whether there's a hoarding problem.

☐ *Your loved one's home has "no access" areas:* People who hoard may close off areas of their homes or try to keep others out of their homes altogether. They may fear that if you see the state of the room or home, you'll demand that they clean the mess, or you'll touch or remove their possessions without their permission. People go to great lengths to keep you out of their spaces. They may tell you that you can't enter a room because it contains unwrapped gifts that they don't want you to see. Other people keep the curtains closed so that others can't see inside their homes. If your loved one tells you that parts of his home are off-limits, or is overly concerned about others seeing inside his home, this may indicate a hoarding problem.

☐ *You and your loved one talk endlessly about the stuff:* A telling sign that a loved one may have a hoarding problem is that you and your loved one talk at great length about the possessions. At first, conversations are gentle and supportive. You might offer suggestions or advice. You might offer to come over on a Saturday to help clear out a few things. Over the years, however, the conversations become louder and more demanding as pleas turn to threats. You may have threatened to call the authorities, and your loved one, in return, may have threatened to never speak to you again. Simply put, if you and your loved one are talking a lot about the stuff, she may have a hoarding problem.

☐ *Your loved one has difficulty throwing things away:* When you ask your loved one why he doesn't discard a few of the plastic bags strewn about the floor, he tells you things like "I can't throw anything away" or "I save everything." Many people who hoard find it easier to donate to charity, to recycle, or to post possessions on online auction sites than to throw things away, and they tell you that that's their plan.

☐ *Your loved one acquires too much and too often:* People who hoard may not admit that they buy things they don't need, in part because they see it quite differently. Without blinking an eye, they tell you that it's always good to have extra presents on hand for unexpected guests or last-minute celebrations.

☐ *Your loved one's home and personal spaces are filled with clutter:* Another sign that your loved may have a hoarding problem may seem obvious: her home and most personal spaces are awash with stuff. We're not talking about the office desk covered with papers or the storage closet filled with umbrellas, coats, and holiday decorations. When we refer to a clutter problem, we mean that it's difficult to walk through a room and to sit in a chair. The person who hoards may not be able to use his shower or tub. He may eat most meals out because he can't get to the stove or oven to prepare meals. He may not be able to drive his automobile because he can no longer sit in the driver's seat or see out the windows.

☐ *Your loved one can't sort, organize, or make decisions about possessions:* An inability to sort possessions efficiently may distinguish the person with a hoarding problem from someone who's only prone to some disorganization and clutter. That is, if a person without hoarding difficulties intentionally carves out three hours to sit down in front of her piles of stuff, she can usually sort and organize these possessions with some level of efficiency. Conversely, the person who hoards likely can't, because he falls into the trap of considering the many and endless ways he can sort, organize, or store an item. Before you know it, the process overwhelms him and he stops.

☐ *Your loved one can't function safely and comfortably in the home:* Some people who hoard have trouble walking through the home because they stumble over floors covered with clutter. This is particularly alarming if the person is frail and uses a cane or walker. Some people who hoard can't leave home quickly in an emergency because they must navigate along paths cut through piles of newspapers, books, or other clutter. They can't walk safely up and down clutter-covered stairs. Some people who hoard can't use the toilet, shower, or tub because they can't get to it or because they don't have running water in the home. Some people who hoard live in a home that's too cold or too hot because the heating or cooling vents are covered with clutter, or because the furnace or air conditioning no longer work. While it's occasionally difficult to distinguish normal saving and cluttering from compulsive hoarding behaviors, a key factor is whether the behaviors pose significant interference in an individual's life. Compulsive hoarding is a clinically significant problem when clutter or saving behaviors interfere with your loved one's ability to live comfortably and safely within her home or if it affects others' ability to do so.

Could It Be Something Else?

Now that you understand the warning signs of compulsive hoarding, let us consider whether your loved one might have a related disorder or condition. First, you may wonder whether your loved one's hoarding problem means that he has obsessive-compulsive disorder (OCD). You may have heard from a medical or mental health provider that hoarding is a form of OCD. This isn't necessarily the case, however.

Hoarding behaviors seem to be independent symptoms. Sometimes they accompany other OCD symptoms, but sometimes they don't. More often, hoarding symptoms accompany a wide range of other psychological conditions, including post-traumatic stress disorder (PTSD), bipolar disorder, brain injury, personality disorders, attention deficit/hyperactivity disorder (ADHD), social phobia, eating disorders, severe self-neglect, and Prader-Willi syndrome (a congenital disorder marked by insatiable hunger and developmental delays).

Therefore, it's best to consider what other problems might be present when there are hoarding symptoms rather than assume that your loved one has OCD. Of particular importance is whether the hoarding symptoms are a sign of dementia or cognitive decline. Many older adults with dementia begin to exhibit hoarding behaviors, often without any history of hoarding behaviors when they were young. It's essential to figure out whether your loved one has dementia or a compulsive hoarding problem without cognitive decline, because the ways to help her would greatly differ if dementia were present.

In sum, hoarding symptoms are a feature of a wide array of psychological and medical syndromes, and may look somewhat different depending on the nature of the underlying problem. Having a hoarding problem does not, in and of itself, indicate that your loved one has OCD. We recommend seeking an evaluation for your loved one if his diagnosis seems fuzzy, as it often will.

In this chapter, you learned about the many factors that contribute to the problem of compulsive hoarding, and hopefully you understand better just how difficult it is for your loved one to let go of a possession. In addition, you have some idea whether your loved one has the problem. In the next chapter, you'll learn about harm reduction, an approach that can help you and your loved one live safely and more comfortably amid the clutter and chaos of her life.

CHAPTER 2

Harm Reduction

As you likely know all too well, the problem of compulsive hoarding isn't easy to solve, in part because many, if not most, of those who suffer from compulsive hoarding don't see that they have a problem. This is perhaps the most frustrating part of the problem for family members. You've likely tried a great many things to no avail, and possibly resigned yourself to walking away from the problem and letting it be. However, letting it be isn't easy to do when you lie awake at night worrying about your loved one's health and safety. You see the risk, the danger, the harm, but what can you do when your loved one refuses help?

This chapter discusses harm reduction, an alternative approach to the problem of compulsive hoarding that recognizes the realities of the condition while offering hope to you and your loved one. We begin the chapter by defining harm reduction and explaining why we think it can help you manage your loved one's hoarding problem. We go on to explain how to apply the principles of harm reduction to this very difficult problem.

What Is Harm Reduction?

Harm reduction is a holistic and humane public health approach (Marlatt 1998). Harm reduction first developed as a way to minimize the risks of intravenous drug use (by providing clean needles) rather than by trying to stop drug use entirely. Smoking-cessation programs, family planning, seat-belt campaigns, school vaccination programs, and health-screening fairs are all examples of public health harm reduction interventions.

Applying Harm Reduction to Compulsive Hoarding

Later in this book, you'll learn how to create a harm reduction plan to manage your loved one's hoarding problem. Before you jump to creating a harm reduction plan, however, we want to mention something that's as important as the plan itself: the attitude with which you carry out the plan. Developers of harm reduction based the approach on a set of principles, values, and assumptions (Denning 2000) that we've applied to the problem of compulsive hoarding. We call this the "harm reduction attitude," which is as important, if not more important, than the harm reduction plan itself.

Principles of Harm Reduction Applied to Compulsive Hoarding

- First, do no harm.
- It's not necessary that your loved one stop all hoarding behavior.
- No two hoarding situations are identical.
- Your loved one is an essential member of the harm reduction team.
- Change is slow.
- Contract failures don't mean that the harm reduction approach is failing.
- Your loved one may have other, more pressing problems than the hoarding problem.

The harm reduction attitude is the compass that guides you and other team members as you apply the harm reduction strategies we describe later in the book.

First, Do No Harm

Abby's mother was eighty-two years old and had lived in her apartment for almost fifty years. The apartment was filled with paper, trash, and rotting food. Abby was worried about her mother's safety and had tried everything to help. Over the years, Abby's mother began to resent

Abby's persistent and loud demands that she clean her apartment until she finally refused to return Abby's calls or hung up when Abby asked about the apartment. One day, after years of threatening her mother, Abby finally told the landlord about her mother's living situation. She was desperate and did it only because she had tried everything else. She hoped that this would frighten her mother into action. Instead, it looked as if even this last-ditch effort to help had failed. Her mother still denied that she had a problem. She still refused all help, and then it appeared as if the landlord would have to evict her—and Abby felt that she was to blame. Abby's last communication from her mother was a postcard. On it her mother had scribbled, "My daughter is dead."

There are risks to everything we do—including helping. In the case of Abby's mother, Abby faced the risks of helping in light of the risks of not helping. However, because she was so intensely worried about her mother, it's possible that she overfocused on the risks of not helping her and lost sight of the risks of helping her solve the hoarding problem. The first principle of harm reduction is to do no harm. By that, we mean that it's essential that you not help in such a way that you cause more harm to your loved one than the hoarding problem itself causes. For example, arguing repeatedly with your loved one such that he refuses to speak to you or any other family members may cause him to withdraw and isolate himself more than the isolation caused by the condition of his home. Removing your loved one from his home when he has nowhere to go because you're worried about his health and safety may cause greater emotional and financial distress for you and your loved one than keeping him in his home and working to minimize the risks he faces.

However, it's not always easy to tell whether you're doing more harm by helping than by not helping. There are risks to both sides of this equation. In the end, perhaps doing no harm means trying, as best you can, to always keep in mind both the risks and benefits of helping. That may be asking a lot of you, but alas, there are no easy solutions to the problem of compulsive hoarding.

It's Not Necessary to Stop All Hoarding Behavior

Harm reduction assumes that it's not necessary that your loved one stop all acquiring or clear all debris to reduce harm. In part, we base this assumption on the obvious fact that it's impossible for any of us to avoid all acquiring and saving. Consider for a moment how your life would look if you didn't bring anything, or only brought a minimal number of things, into your home: one set of clothing, one box of tissue, one chair to sit on. Harm reduction assumes the attitude that any step in the right direction is a good one (Marlatt and Tapert 1993). The goal is to help your loved one make positive changes in her life, even though she continues to engage in some hoarding behavior.

No Two Hoarding Situations Are Identical

Biological, cultural, ethnic, and social influences, as well as a person's unique environment and history, likely all contribute to the development of a serious and persistent compulsive hoarding problem. For example, cultural or ethnic variables may influence the degree to which family members or communities view extreme saving or frugality as traits to be valued. Whether someone has a little money or a lot can influence what and how much he compulsively acquires. Someone with many children who visit her frequently may save a bit less because her family members encourage her to refrain from acquiring, whereas a person who lives alone and without social contact may have nothing to restrain her urges to acquire and save.

Harm reduction assumes that each hoarding situation is unique and that therefore no two harm reduction plans are the same. This attitude encourages you and other members of the harm reduction team to develop a plan that's reasonable and achievable for your loved one's unique hoarding situation.

Your Loved One Is an Essential Member of the Harm Reduction Team

Harm reduction assumes that your loved one has the right to make choices and, as such, to participate in solving his hoarding problem. If your loved one has some say in how harm reduction proceeds, he's likely to be a bit less anxious and more open to accepting help. Even with harm reduction, you're asking a great deal from your loved one. You're asking him to set aside his fears, mistrust, and resentment to try something he hasn't tried before. Harm reduction can help with all of this, but not if your loved one feels that you're doing harm reduction "to him" rather than "with him."

In addition, people who hoard often have creative harm reduction solutions. Many times, you'll discover that your loved one comes up with a harm reduction strategy that never occurred to anyone else on the harm reduction team. In addition, your loved one is much more likely to follow her own advice than yours and do what she has suggested rather than what you've suggested. Last, sitting around a table with your loved one, working together toward the shared goal of helping her to live safely and comfortably in her home, begins the process of rebuilding trust and reconnecting with each other.

Change Is Slow

If you've tried to change a habit, you know just how difficult that can be sometimes. Perhaps you've tried to stop smoking or start exercising regularly. Change is slow. Now, think about the problem of compulsive hoarding. Your loved one may have been hoarding for thirty, forty, or fifty years, doing the same little things over and over again. Changing hoarding behavior, even in small ways, is very difficult, and the longer your loved one has been hoarding, the more difficult it will be for him to change. At times, you'll wonder whether you're helping, because the changes you see are achingly small. However, any step in the right direction counts as success in harm reduction (Marlatt 1996).

Contract Failures Don't Mean That the Harm Reduction Approach Has Failed

Later in this book, you'll learn how to create a harm reduction contract that formalizes the particular features of the harm reduction plan you devised for your loved one. However, just because your loved one has signed her harm reduction contract doesn't mean that she'll always honor it. Harm reduction assumes that people who compulsively hoard have varying levels of interest and motivation to work on the hoarding problem and that this interest and motivation changes from day to day and often from moment to moment. This means that contract failures are inevitable. In fact, how you and other members of the harm reduction team handle contract failures is more important than preventing contract failures altogether.

Your Loved One May Have Other, More Pressing Problems

The harm reduction approach acknowledges that your loved one may have other, more pressing problems than compulsive hoarding. He may be facing eviction and soon be out on the street if you don't solve the hoarding problem quickly and effectively. Your loved one may be depressed and, for that reason, have trouble working or doing simple tasks like bathing or eating. Your loved one may have health problems, such as heart disease or dementia, that make it difficult for her to work on the hoarding problem or simply to get around in her house. Your loved one may be in an abusive relationship with a spouse, or simply unable or unwilling to reach out to family members or friends. Your loved one's hoarding problem may have caused some of these problems, or perhaps these problems preceded the hoarding problem but now make the hoarding problem worse. Many times, your loved one will accept help for one of these problems while continuing to refuse help for the hoarding problem itself. Harm reduction views these more pressing problems as opportunities to help your loved one accept help. As you'll see in chapter 6, an effective harm reduction plan includes your loved one's most urgent concerns. Including your loved one in the process of clarifying and setting harm reduction goals is likely to mean that he's more inclined to participate in the harm reduction approach.

Why Harm Reduction Can Help

If your loved one has little or no insight about her hoarding problem and therefore isn't open to treatment, and lives in a home that's unsafe and unhealthy, harm reduction may be the logical choice. This section outlines the reasons why you and your loved one may want to consider harm reduction as a way to manage the hoarding problem.

Most People Who Hoard Refuse Help

Many of those who suffer with compulsive hoarding seldom seek or accept treatment or help for the problem, either because they don't see that they have a problem or because they fear discovery by landlords who might evict them, officials who might condemn their homes, or family members who might discard their possessions. When they do accept help, it's often because they face eviction or can no longer live safely in their homes. In addition, for the few who seek or agree to treatment, the effectiveness of current approaches (whether medication or psychotherapy) is low, while relapse rates are high (Frost and Steketee 1998). Harm reduction is an alternative approach for those who refuse treatment or, at best, don't respond as well or as quickly as necessary. Harm reduction may be the only hope for your loved one if he repeatedly refuses all help and continues to live in unsafe conditions.

Significant Risks to the Person with the Hoarding Problem

Compulsive hoarding places your loved one at risk as long as she continues to compulsively acquire and save. Many people who hoard are unable to sleep in their beds or sit at their dining tables. About half of those who suffer with compulsive hoarding are unable to use the stove top, refrigerator, or tub or sink, and one in ten is unable to use the toilet (Frost, Steketee, and Williams 2000). Often people who hoard can't heat or cool their homes, because clutter blocks the heating or cooling vents. Their homes are often in disrepair, because they won't let anyone into their homes to repair the roof, sink, or toilet out of shame or fear of discovery. Harm reduction recognizes the significant risks your loved one faces daily and focuses on minimizing these risks in a variety of creative ways.

Significant Risks to Family Members and Communities

Compulsive hoarding not only affects your loved one's mental, emotional, and physical health, but also your own and that of other members of the community in which he lives. The problem of hoarding devastates families and friendships, irrevocably damaging once close and intimate relationships. Compulsive hoarding affects the neighborhood, township, and municipality in which your loved one lives. The problem raises many and varied health and safety concerns for communities, and can involve a multitude of agencies and organizations (for example, elder services, fire and police departments, animal rescue, child and adult protective services, and housing-advocacy organizations). The estimated costs of dealing with the problem are huge, whether the costs of direct mental health or support services to people who hoard or the costs of clearing homes (Tolin et al. 2008). Because people who hoard have suffered with the problem for decades, sometimes fifty or sixty years, by the time authorities discover the problem, it's often cheaper to bulldoze the home than to clear it. Thus, authorities must force older adults, many in frail and failing health, from their homes at the most vulnerable of times. Harm reduction recognizes the significant harm that family members and communities face, and strives to minimize rather than eliminate harm to all those affected by this devastating problem.

Overfocusing on Treatment or Discarding Can Make Things Worse

When you overfocus on treatment or on discarding possessions, you run the risk of alienating your loved one and thereby decrease the likelihood that she'll accept help of any kind. Over the years, you've likely tried to help, perhaps by haranguing your loved one to get help or treatment for the hoarding problem or demanding that he throw things out, or when he has been out of his home, discarding a few things yourself. Your loved one likely reacted to your help with outrage and anger, which only adds to the frustration, hopelessness, and fear you feel. An overemphasis on clearing homes and discarding possessions may limit the number of those with a hoarding problem who accept help. Harm reduction emphasizes living safely and comfortably over living with fewer possessions and thereby is a more pragmatic alternative for you and your loved one.

The Need for Ongoing Monitoring and Assistance

Most instances of compulsive hoarding require ongoing monitoring and help, even for those who benefited from treatment. For those who reject treatment but permit, or are forced to accept, clear-out interventions (either staged by families or officials), few are able to keep their homes clear without ongoing assistance. Harm reduction takes the long view about the problem of compulsive hoarding and focuses on helping your loved one live safely and comfortably in her home as long as she lives there.

In this chapter, you learned about harm reduction and why this approach to the problem of hoarding might help. In addition, you learned a set of guiding principles and assumptions that we call the "harm reduction attitude." The harm reduction attitude is perhaps the most important feature of an effective harm reduction approach and guides everything that follows. In particular, if you hope to help your loved one accept a harm reduction plan, he must see that you have a harm reduction attitude and that you truly believe in it. In the next chapter, you'll learn how to set the stage for harm reduction, which begins with letting go and rests on understanding and forgiveness.

CHAPTER 3

Setting the Stage for Harm Reduction

Like most things, there are at least two sides to every story. Let us hear Jeff's side of the story first. Jeff is fifty-three years old, and his father, Clarence, is seventy-seven. Jeff speaks with pride about how his father could build or fix anything, and how they spent many weekends building birdhouses and repairing anything with an engine. Today, however, Jeff is bitter and angry, and after years of arguing with his father, he's given up.

> *My father is stubborn and impossible. His house is a dump because he never—and I mean never—throws anything out. "I'm going to fix it someday," he says. He used to tell me that he would repair the stuff when he retired and had more time. He's been retired for twelve years now, and he's still telling me he'll get around to it. Now, he has so much junk, he can't even walk around in the house. He's fallen three or four times. He bathes at the sink because he can't use the shower or tub. It's horrible, and I'm too ashamed to tell anyone. My wife knows, of course, but we haven't told our kids. They haven't been over to their granddad's house in two or three years because my wife thinks the house isn't safe, and she's right. Over the years, I've tried to help him clear a few things out, but now he won't even let me into the house. I call him, but he doesn't call back. I'm at the stage now where if I don't give up, I'm going to go crazy with worry.*

Clarence has a different story. He no longer speaks to his son because he feels hurt and betrayed. One day, Jeff tells him he's worried about him, and then the next day, he threatens to turn him in to the fire department. Clarence is lonely and confused. Sometimes he thinks about clearing a few things out so that his grandkids could visit, but he's too hurt and bitter to ask Jeff for help.

I don't care what he says; he can't tell me what to do with my stuff. He says he's worried about me, but you couldn't prove it by me. He's threatened to call the cops or the fire department, because he says my house is a firetrap. If he were really worried about me, he wouldn't threaten to have his own father thrown out on the street. He's become obsessed with getting rid of my stuff, and I don't get it. We used to have a great time together when he was a kid. We'd build things in my shop, and he seemed to enjoy looking through my tools and other stuff. Now, all he talks about his throwing stuff away. The worst part, though, is that he won't let me see my own grandkids. He says my place isn't safe for them. I don't know if I can ever forgive Jeff for taking them away from me.

Jeff and Clarence are stuck. Neither can let go, neither can understand, and neither can forgive. As long as they're stuck, they can't move ahead with the approach we outline in this book. Setting the stage may be the most difficult thing we ask of you, because it's all about what you do, not what your loved one does.

Let Go

Over the years, you've likely urged, cajoled, and perhaps harangued your loved one to let go of her stuff. You may have even threatened to call the fire department or the police in the hope that she would let go of just a few things. Instead, rather than letting go of stuff, she seems to hold on tighter to the possessions she has. Yes, your loved one has trouble letting go. However, we think that many family members also have trouble letting go. For you, it's not that you can't let go of too many bags, boxes, shoes, or magazines. For you, it's that you can't let go of the past hurts, lingering resentments, and ongoing fear and worry. To help your loved one, we must first help you let go of the emotional baggage that weighs you down and stands in the way of your reconnecting with your loved one and helping him in a new way.

Let Go of Past Hurts and Misunderstandings

Yes, you've been hurt too. Perhaps the most hurtful thing about hoarding is that family members feel second to their loved one's possessions. Family members tell us that they missed birthday parties as kids because their parent lost the invitations in the junk. They couldn't have sleepovers at their homes and never brought anyone over—friend, boyfriend or girlfriend, coach, or teacher—because of the stuff. They've told us that they never had a family gathering at home during the holidays because it stressed out their mother or father.

In addition to the hurt family members feel about having missed the things other people take for granted, you may also remember how you were hurt when you tried to help. There may have been times when you tried to help by taking a few possessions away, and your loved one thanked you by calling you a thief or a liar. Perhaps you've called your loved one worse, and now you feel bad about that.

Last, you may have struggled, and perhaps still struggle, with your own shame and embarrassment because of the way your loved one lives. Letting go of the shame and embarrassment you feel is sometimes the hardest thing to let go of. For some people, it's easier to let go of their anger, resentment, and even hurt—but the shame lingers on and haunts their relationship with their loved one. Glenn remembers growing up acting as if he lived in another neighborhood. When a classmate's parent drove him home from school or a sporting event, he asked the parent to drop him off at the corner down the block so no one would know where he lived. When a parent insisted on dropping him off at home, he would direct the neighbor to a house down the street. When the car stopped in front of the house, Glenn would step out of the car and walk up the path to the house, turning back to smile and wave as the parent drove away. Glenn remembers the shame as if it were yesterday.

Let Go of What You Think Will Make Your Loved One Happy

Over the years, we've met many family members who were certain they knew what would make their loved ones who hoard happy: less clutter, a cleaner and neater home, running water, a roof that doesn't leak. They looked at us and told us to talk to their loved ones and try to make them understand that they're not happy—they couldn't be and still live the way they do.

We all have beliefs concerning what's right and what's wrong about the way people live. Some of us are more comfortable with clutter than others. You may share an office with a coworker who has layered his desk with papers, folders, pens, and pencils and wonder how he can work, how he can find anything. You may shake your head when you pass the overgrown lawn or faded paint on a neighbor's house and think that she must not have much pride in herself or the way she lives. To help your loved one, it's important to let go of many of your beliefs about the importance of possessions, about the best way to live, and about how clean is clean enough.

Let Go of Helping Without Your Loved One's Permission

If you're like most family members, the hardest part of loving someone who hoards is that he often, if not always, refuses your help. You've learned some reasons for this. Still, this reality is one of the most frustrating and demoralizing aspects of having a loved one who compulsively hoards. You've likely argued, cajoled, pleaded, and threatened your loved one for many years—and you both remain stuck.

You might think that letting go of the hope that you can help is the same as giving up. This isn't true. You can still help, but only if you recognize that you can't do that without the participation of your loved one, in some way. Many family members tell us that they let go years ago, but it didn't work because their loved one didn't change. However, this isn't really letting go if you do it in order to get your loved one to change or come around to your way of thinking and living. Instead, letting go is what we do when we can't do anything more.

The harm reduction approach described in this book will work as long as you and your loved one are committed to working together through the ups and downs, and through the hurts and misunderstandings. And we assure you that there'll be more hurts and misunderstandings as you dig out. We encourage you to let go of those too. Letting go will help you and your loved one keep going, because then you may feel a little less like wanting to give up.

Let Go

Although letting go is a very difficult and complicated journey, it begins with the first step. Try the following exercise and see if it helps you begin to let go. Here's a word of advice: This exercise is for you, not your loved one. You may think that your loved one needs to let go of a few things too, such as the resentment or mistrust she holds against you. This may be true, but you can't *make* your loved one let go. Furthermore, trying to get her to let go has, in part, brought you here. It's better if each family member completes this exercise alone to avoid turning the process of letting go into a bashing session against your loved one. Perhaps later, if you wish, you might share what you've written with other family members, but this is really for you, not for your loved one or other family members.

Take out a piece of paper or a notebook. Write out your past hurts and the many things you think are right, or what you think your loved one should do. Write what you thought you would never tell anyone out of fear that you would hurt your loved one or that no one would understand.

- What has your loved one done that has hurt you the most, and how do you feel about that? What things have you done to help that your loved one has misunderstood and felt angry about? How do you feel about these misunderstandings?

- What do you think would make your loved one happy? What do you think your loved one should do to be happier? Has your loved one done these things? If not, how do you feel about that?

- How do you think your loved one should live? How do you feel about your loved one's refusal to live that way?

- Have you tried to help your loved one without his permission? What happened, and how did that make you feel? How have you tried to help in the past, and how did your loved one react to you? How do you feel when people try to help you without your permission?

Understand

The problem of compulsive hoarding is difficult to understand. Many times, you would never guess that someone has the problem. They hold jobs. They dress neatly and are responsible citizens. You've likely chatted with them at parties or stood behind them in line at the bank or grocery. In many ways, they're just like you—except they're not.

In chapter 1, we described what we currently know about the condition, but still, most researchers (and family members) see it as a puzzle with too many missing pieces. The reality is that you may never fully understand why your loved one saves to excess and can never let anything go. However, we hope that by now you understand your loved one's hoarding problem in a different way. We hope that you no longer see the problem as if your loved one is lazy or dirty, or cares more about things than about you. This way of understanding is neither true nor helpful.

Forgive

In this section, we encourage you to consider two things, both of which have to do with forgiveness. First, we encourage you to forgive your loved one. This is not an easy thing, but you can do it if you want. If forgiving your loved one sounds difficult, consider the second thing we ask you to do: seek forgiveness from your loved one. Forgiving and seeking forgiveness are processes, each with its own twists and turns. However, until you and your loved one forgive each other to some degree, you may not be able to move to the next step of creating a harm reduction plan and managing the hoarding problem together. Forgiveness is an essential step in the process of harm reduction and, perhaps, the most difficult.

We begin with your learning to forgive. If you have a therapist, counselor, or someone to whom you look for advice and help, this would be the time to reconnect with that person. Suggest that this person help you through the process of forgiving your loved one. If you aren't seeing a therapist, this might be the time to begin. Forgiving isn't easy, but it's healing and it's for you. Not forgiving hurts you the most. In addition, you won't be able to fully participate in the harm reduction approach and participate effectively as a team member until you've forgiven.

Forgive Your Loved One

Kathleen is stuck. She wants to help her mother, but she's not sure she can forgive her for the many things she suffered because of her mother's hoarding problem—and she did suffer, and suffers still. Kathleen never finished college and has worked at a series of jobs that she feels haven't matched her capabilities. Her view is that this is her mother's fault, because she believes her mother cared more about her stuff than about Kathleen's progress in school. Kathleen doesn't have as many friends as she would like and sees this as her mother's fault too. She believes that if she had been able to bring more friends to the house when she was a kid, she wouldn't struggle as much with making friends now. Kathleen is also depressed and believes that she would be happier if her mother had focused less on her stuff and more on her.

In his popular book *Forgive for Good*, Fred Luskin writes (2002) that we have trouble forgiving when we take something too personally, when we continue blaming the person who hurt us for how bad we feel, and when we create a grievance story. According to Luskin, the grievance process begins when something happens that we don't like and we continue thinking about it too much and for too long. Luskin refers to this as renting the hurt and disappointment too much space in your mind. Forgiveness, then, is the antidote to the grievance and opens the door to greater personal peace. However, forgiveness is difficult, in part because we must work through several obstacles.

You may confuse your inability to forgive with an unforgivable offense. Perhaps the single largest roadblock to forgiving your loved one is the belief that what he did to you is unforgiveable. People tell us that they would forgive the person if they could, but they can't because the offense is just too big. Ask yourself, "Could I forgive my loved one if someone gave me fifty million dollars to put all the grievances out of my mind?" Alternatively, what if you had a life-threatening illness and the only way to save yourself was to forgive your loved one. Could you do it? Could you forgive your loved one to earn fifty million dollars? Could you forgive her to save your life? In a sense, forgiving has the potential to bring you many rewards. Do you want to live, or do you want to suffer for the privilege of remaining hurt and angry?

You may not know how to forgive. Often, people want to forgive and believe they can do it. They just don't know how. We know that people can forgive. If you look around, you may know some who have forgiven the very same offense. If you lack the tools to forgive, the task may feel overwhelming. You may not know how to begin. You may even wonder whether it's possible to learn to forgive or whether someone can teach you.

You keep doing what doesn't work. A final obstacle to forgiveness is that we continue to react to hurt and disappointment in ways that don't work. You've likely tried many strategies to avoid being hurt or disappointed.

Perhaps you've avoided the topic of hoarding altogether or cut your loved one out of your life. Some solutions may have worked better than others. For example, for years, Jack's father complained about the clutter in his home but refused Jack's offers to help. This frustrated and hurt Jack. On several occasions, Jack resolved that he wouldn't offer to help his father clean his home unless his father asked. Jack tried that for a while, but after several months, he fell back into his old pattern of offering to help when his father complained, only to be hurt again when his father refused. Reacting in the same fruitless way is an obstacle to forgiveness in that it gets in the way of our trying new solutions to the hoarding problem. You may want to make a list of everything you've tried to solve your loved one's hoarding problem and of the grievances that have built over the years when you've tried to help and been hurt. Place a check mark next to the ones that have failed. Perhaps you're ready to try something new: forgiveness.

Forgiveness is a skill that you can learn and practice, like learning to ride a bike. You might think, "Yes, I'm willing to try to forgive my loved one if it's the only way to help her." However, true forgiveness is for you and not for your loved one. We'll come to your loved one later, when we describe the importance of seeking his forgiveness in order to set the stage for all that follows. For now, however, we're asking you to forgive. It's in your control. You have a choice and can choose to change the way you feel. Forgiveness is about your healing, not about the loved one who hurt you.

We don't have the space to teach you all the tools available to those who want to learn to forgive. Check out Luskin's book and others in our appendix for additional information that can help you forgive your loved one. For now, HEAL is a powerful tool that we've adapted with permission (Luskin 2002); learn how to use it in the following exercise.

HEAL

This exercise will help you begin the process of forgiving and healing. Take out a piece of paper or a notebook. Write your own HEAL—hope, educate, affirm, and long-term—statements for a specific situation for which you're having trouble forgiving your loved one. Focus on the effects of the hoarding problem on your life.

1. **Hope:** A statement expressed as a wish, preference, or hope. The Hope statement is a positive and personal desire for a specific outcome in a specific situation, but it doesn't express a hope that your loved one

will change. Focus on what you wanted to happen rather than what you didn't want to happen; for example, "I wanted to have a childhood like my friends" or "I wanted my mother to care about me the way she cared about her possessions."

2. **Educate:** A reminder that you can't truly control your loved one, yourself, or life events. The Educate statement describes the world in the way it operates, and acknowledges that you fully accept that reality. This statement is an impersonal recognition that you may not get what you want, even though you're a good person. You may not get what you want, and you might get something better or worse; for example, "Even though I wanted to have a childhood like my friends, I understand and accept that it was different" or "Even though I wanted my mother to care about me, I understand and accept that she didn't care about me as much as I wanted."

3. **Affirm:** Your positive intention to reconnect with and move forward with the life goals that your hurts and disappointments have pushed aside. Your positive intention reconnects you to your big dreams and deepest hopes, and permits you to mourn your losses. It reorients you to your growth and development as a person; for example, "I want to be the best parent I can to my own children" or "I want to fill my life with good people who care about me and others."

4. **Long-term:** An emphasis on the importance of practicing forgiveness every day, whether you feel hurt or upset about a past or present event. This statement reminds you that each day presents you with new opportunities to practice forgiveness. Since you'll slip back into your old patterns from time to time, it can help to ask a trusted friend or family member to remind you to HEAL when you're back in your old grievance story. Find people who have successfully forgiven others who've hurt them. Listen to what they have to say. At times, you won't be able to set aside the grievance. Go ahead and give yourself permission to mull over the grievance for a short period, perhaps fifteen minutes, and then move on with your life. Affirm, "I make a long-term commitment to learn all that I need in order to heal fully."

Seek Forgiveness from Your Loved One

At this point, you may see the value of letting go of your hurt and anger. You may see the value of understanding the hoarding problem through the eyes of your loved one. You may even be willing to forgive your loved one for the lost years or the unkind things he has said to you. You may think that this is enough. However, we're about to ask more from you and perhaps ask you to try the most challenging task yet. We're about to ask you to seek forgiveness from your loved one: to ask your loved one to forgive you.

Seeking forgiveness sets the stage for harm reduction, because past resentments, hurts, and suspicions are major roadblocks to your and your loved one's working together in this new way. You may think, "What do I have to apologize for? I was only trying to help!" or "Look, I admit I've made mistakes, but how about her apologizing for the hell she put me through? When does she ask for my forgiveness?" Seeking forgiveness is not a quid pro quo agreement: "I'll forgive when he does." Seeking forgiveness is not a way to get something from your loved one: "I'll forgive because I want her to forgive me too." To seek true forgiveness means that we seek it with no expectation that our loved one will seek our forgiveness too. This may happen, but then again, it may not. We don't bargain with forgiveness.

Decide who will begin the process. Sometimes, the best person to begin the process of seeking forgiveness is the family member who has some contact with your loved one. There are many reasons for this. Perhaps your loved one has always been more comfortable or a bit less angry or resentful with this family member. If that's the case, ask this family member to begin the process and work toward opening the door so that other family members can seek your loved one's forgiveness. Encourage the family member who begins the process to listen to your loved one rather than feel pressured to defend the actions of the other family members. Listening, empathizing, and encouraging your loved one to meet with other family members so that they can hear him out is the best strategy.

It's important that the family member who agrees to begin the process of seeking forgiveness understand a couple of important things. First, setting the stage by forgiving and seeking forgiveness is essential if harm reduction is to work. Some family members want to get right to "helping" their loved one and don't see that their loved one may continue to refuse their help if they don't complete this first step. In addition, it's essential that the family member who agrees to start the process have the temperament for this job. Seeking forgiveness takes patience, energy, and a willingness to hear, without becoming defensive, your loved one tell you how much you've hurt her and why what you did was wrong.

If you have current contact with your loved one, follow these steps. If you or another family member has some contact with your loved one, you're ahead of the game. The door's already open, if only a bit. We recommend that you build on this by increasing the number of visits you make to your loved one's home, even if it's only to stop by and say hello. However, during these visits, don't bring up the hoarding problem. Mix social visits in your loved one's home with fun outings, but always come back for a bit of time in his home. The goal of these visits is twofold. First, we want you to increase positive feelings between you and your loved one, thereby building some trust and comfort. Over the years, even during social visits, you've likely ended up talking about your loved one's hoarding problem, and these discussions may have ended in intense arguments. Second, we want your loved one to reattach to you and to the benefits of loving and caring relationships with her family. As we mentioned, people change when they have reasons to change. However, too often, family members believe that their loved one should change so that she can live in a clean and uncluttered environment. In our experience, this argument seldom wins the day. Instead, people with a hoarding problem are more open to change when they can have more of what they value, which is what most of us value: time with a loving and caring family.

If you don't have current contact with your loved one, follow these steps. At times, a loved one has closed the door to any contact from you or other family members. He refuses to let you into his home. He doesn't return your calls, e-mails, or letters. At other times, however, it's you or other family members who've closed the door. Children, brothers, sisters, and friends no longer speak to or see the person who hoards, because they've given up after years of reaching out and being rebuked, or they're too hurt and angry to want to try. If you or other family members don't see or speak to your loved one, you must begin to reach out in small ways. Write simple hellos, send postcards, and call and leave voice-mail messages. Start by saying that you hope she's feeling well. Invite her to call or write you. Leave a bag of food on the doorstep. After a time, include a brief remark stating that you hope your loved one will forgive you, but always ask for a face-to-face meeting at some point. Ask your loved one to consider opening the door. Keep going until your loved one says yes, and when he does, follow the four A's to forgiveness.

Four A's to Forgiveness

There are four A's to seeking forgiveness from your loved one: (1) acknowledge that your loved one feels betrayed by you and other family members; (2) assign reasons by explaining why you did what you did; (3) assure your loved one that from now on, things will be different; and (4) ask your loved one to forgive you.

Acknowledge. It's natural to think you had to do what you did, whether it was throwing some things out, trying to frighten your loved one into action by calling the authorities, or pleading with her to accept some help. More than anything, you were worried about her safety and health. You were only trying to help. However, your loved one likely feels hurt, betrayed, and confused. It's essential that you acknowledge these feelings. Let your loved one know that you regret having tried to help in this way, and admit that it didn't work. Don't deny that your loved one feels what he feels. Don't tell him to get over it or that he's making too big a deal of it. Don't become defensive and tell her that you did it for her own good. Don't blame her or say that she forced you to do it. Ask her to tell you how she felt when you did this or that. Give her some specific examples of the things you did that you now regret, and solicit from her other past grievances.

Assign reasons. Now, explain why you did what you did, but don't make excuses. Emphasize that you did it because you were afraid or felt bad because your loved one was sometimes cold or hungry. Explain your reasons for acting, and tell your loved one how you thought it through. However, don't expect him to agree with your reasoning. In fact, expect him to disagree, and say back to him, "I'm sorry that I threw away some of your things without asking you first. I felt frustrated and worried about the way you live. I can hear that you're upset with me and that you don't see it the way I see it. I understand that we see it differently. I get that now. I'm sorry." Ask him only to understand why you did it, not agree that you were right or correct.

Tell your loved one that now you can see that she wasn't as worried as you were, or that you and she didn't see the situation in the same way. Take care not to say this in a way that implies to your loved one that she should've been more worried or anxious, and that's why you did it. This sends the message that you were right and she was wrong. It sounds a lot like an excuse. Although you may be correct that your loved one is unsafe, being correct can get in the way of obtaining your loved one's forgiveness. In addition, don't ask her to accept your reasons but to understand why you did what you did. "I did it because I care about you, and it breaks my heart to see you living like this, but now I see the harm I've done to our relationship. I hope you can understand why I did it, although I accept that you may not."

Assure your loved one that it'll be different now. Tell your loved one that it won't happen this way again. Tell him that from now on, you won't touch his things without his permission. You won't discard or move things unless he asks you to do it first. You won't argue with him or threaten to call the authorities, nor will you try to get him to see things your way. However, don't promise these things unless you're certain that you can deliver. Explain to him that you're there to help in another way when he's ready and willing to listen. If your loved one asks about the other way of helping that you have in mind, you can introduce the idea of harm reduction (see chapter 4) but not before he has truly forgiven you.

Ask for forgiveness. In asking for forgiveness, you're asking your loved one to try to understand (not accept as correct) why you did what you did, how much you care about your loved one, and how much her forgiveness means to you. Don't fall back into the pattern of defending your actions. Don't react. Don't argue. Don't tell your loved one that she was wrong too; only repeat why you did what you did: "I was afraid. I desperately wanted to do something to help, because I care about you. I'm sorry. Now I see that what I did wasn't helpful at all."

Don't expect your loved one to forgive you right away. This may take many discussions with many people in your family. Above all, be patient. If during a conversation your loved one doesn't forgive you, thank him for listening. After every conversation, whether successful or not, write a letter to your loved one outlining what you heard him say. In the letter, make certain to tell him that this is what you heard but that you could have heard wrong. Even if a conversation is unsuccessful, writing a letter like this communicates to your loved one that you were listening.

TIPS FOR SEEKING FORGIVENESS

■ Select the best family member to begin the process.

■ Start with simple social visits to build trust and increase positive interactions.

■ Introduce other family members in stages but always with your loved one's permission.

■ Don't offer to help with the hoarding problem; try to talk about something else.

■ Find value in some of your loved one's possessions and seek common ground.

■ Send letters, postcards, and small acts of kindness to open the door.

■ Prepare yourself to hear your loved one express her hurt and anger.

■ When the time comes to seek forgiveness, use the four A's and prepare ahead of time.

DO'S AND DON'TS OF FORGIVENESS

Do	Don't
Do acknowledge your loved one's feelings of hurt, anger, fear, and betrayal.	*Don't* deny your loved one's feelings of hurt, anger, fear, and betrayal.
Do explain why you did what you did.	*Don't* expect that your loved one will forgive you right away.
Do be honest about how you felt and what you did.	*Don't* blame your loved one for what you felt you had to do.
Do ask your loved one to forgive you.	*Don't* make excuses for what you did or say that you had to do it (unless this is true).

Preparing to Seek Forgiveness

In this exercise, we guide you through the process of preparing to seek forgiveness from your loved one. We suggest that you develop a seeking-forgiveness script that you can use when speaking to your loved one. Seeking forgiveness can bring up strong emotions for you and your loved one. The more prepared you are, the more likely that you'll be able to hold the course in the face of your loved one's anger and suspiciousness, and your own anxiety and guilt.

Take out a piece of paper or a notebook. Draw two columns on the paper. In the left-hand column, write each of the four A's:

■ *Acknowledge* your loved one's feelings of hurt, anger, and betrayal.

■ *Assign* reasons for what you did, but don't make excuses.

■ *Assure* your loved one that you want to help in different ways.

■ *Ask* for your loved one to forgive you.

In the right-hand column, write clear and brief statements to your loved one for each of the four A's. Once you have your script, read it to a neutral, objective friend or family member to make certain that the tone of the message isn't blaming or defensive. In addition, remember that forgiveness takes time.

Grab Hold

We're asking you to let go, but what, you might ask, are we encouraging you to grab hold of in the storm of past hurt, misunderstanding, and resentment, and in the current storm of fear, worry, and guilt? The answer is to refocus on the good parts of the relationship with your loved one. Most, if not all, relationships are a mixture of good and bad parts. Over the years, you and your loved one likely have overfocused on the "bad" parts of your relationship, that is, on the many arguments and disagreements about the stuff. Rather than continuing to try to rescue your loved one from his possessions, we suggest, instead, that you try to recapture what you value or once valued about your relationship with your loved one.

Grab Hold

Take out a notebook or a piece of paper. Think about how you would like your relationship with your loved one to look, rather than how you would like his house to look. Write down your thoughts and feelings about the good parts of the relationship with your loved one. Perhaps you once enjoyed doing things together. What were those things? What qualities (interests, passions, or quirks) about your loved one did you once value and cherish? What are your fondest memories with your loved one? What things about your relationship with your loved one do you miss? What things about your relationship with your loved one do you want back?

In this chapter, you learned how to set the stage for harm reduction by letting go of past hurts and what you think will make your loved one happy. In addition, you've accepted that you can't help your loved one without her permission, which opens the door to finding ways to understand and forgive. Finally, you've identified what you can grab hold of in your relationship with your loved one as you try to help in a new way. The following chapter presents strategies for helping your loved one accept help, in particular to accept help in the form of a harm reduction plan to manage her hoarding problem.

CHAPTER 4

Helping Them Accept Help

If you're like most family members with a loved one who hoards, you're bewildered by both the hoarding problem itself and (perhaps even more) by your loved one's unwillingness to accept help. As you learned in the introduction, people who hoard refuse help for a number of reasons. Regardless of the reasons, you still want to help. That's clear. "But how?" you might ask yourself. "How do I help my loved one accept help?"

In this chapter, we describe strategies you can use to help your loved one accept help. Your loved one may be more open to a harm reduction approach than to other options you may have tried, particularly if she has limited insight about her hoarding problem. If you find that your loved one isn't even open to this approach, you may not have yet set the stage, as we described in chapter 3. Therefore, make sure you've completed this essential preparatory work before moving to the next step in your plan to help your loved one.

Engaging Your Loved One in the Harm Reduction Approach

In this section, we take up the topic of how to engage your loved one in the harm reduction approach. We know that you've repeatedly tried to convince your loved one to accept help and dealt with his indifference or repeated refusals. However, we think it can be different for you and your loved one this time for several reasons.

First, you've set the stage by forgiving and seeking forgiveness from your loved one. We know that this wasn't easy, but in so doing, you've set new expectations for you and your loved one. Second, you're setting realistic goals that focus on having your loved one live safely and comfortably in her home. You're not seeking treatment for her or chang-ing radically the way she chooses to live. Last, because harm reduction doesn't overfocus on discarding, you may discover that your loved one is more open to receiving your help. However, because harm reduction is for those who have little or no insight about their hoarding problems, we don't expect that it will be an easy sell, perhaps just a bit easier to sell than what you've tried in the past.

L.E.A.P.: Listen, Empathize, Agree, and Partner

Learning to work with your loved one's persistent refusal to accept help for his hoarding problem is perhaps the single most important thing you'll learn in this book. We've adapted an approach developed by Xavier Amador in his popular book, *I Am Not Sick, I Don't Need Help! Helping the Seriously Mentally Ill Accept Treatment: A Practical Guide for Families and Therapists* (2000, 51–107; by permission of Vida Press, Peconic, New York). The approach includes four steps—L.E.A.P.: listening, empathiz-ing, agreeing, and partnering—that you can use to help your loved one accept help for his hoarding problem. We recommend using L.E.A.P. to engage and reengage your loved one in the harm reduction approach. We say "reengage," because helping your loved one accept help is an ongoing process. Even after you've set up and been working on your loved one's harm reduction plan for a while, his willingness to accept help will ebb and flow. At those times, we recommend shifting to L.E.A.P. to reengage your loved one in the harm reduction plan and renew his motivation to work with you on the hoarding problem.

LISTENING

You might think you're a good listener. You might say, "I listen to my loved one. I hear what she's saying." Listening, however, is more than hearing what your loved one says. Real listening means that you set aside your own assumptions, interests, and needs with the goal of learning about your loved one. Real listening says to your loved one, "I'm interested in you. I want to know what you think and feel." When you're really listening, you're engaged in the process. Real listening isn't passive listening, whereby you sit back and let your loved one's words wash over you without comment or attention. Real listening is active listen-ing (Rogers 1951), in which you fully participate, even if your loved one does all the talking. When you're actively listening, you're engaged in paraphrasing, clarifying, and giving feedback in order to get the message right.

Paraphrasing: To paraphrase, you open with a declaration of what you heard but let your loved one know that it's possible that you heard wrong. You can say, "What I hear you saying is…," "If I heard you right, you said…," or "I really want to get this straight; you said…" You can even say, "I may have misunderstood you, but I thought you said…" You may have your favorite way of opening, and it's okay to use several of these openers throughout a conversation. Often, paraphrasing works best when you thoughtfully rephrase what your loved one said, while communicating that you may have misunderstood. Look at how Ted paraphrased when talking to his mother about accepting help for her hoarding problem:

Ted: "Mom, I'd like to talk to you about a way I can help with the hoarding problem."

Laura: "I've told you. I don't need any help. My house is fine. I'm fine. I don't understand why you think I need help."

Ted: "You've told me repeatedly that you don't want my help."

Laura: "Yes. I don't see why I can't live the way I want. I'm not bothering anybody."

Ted: "I hear you saying that you're not bothering anyone and that you don't like people nagging you about the way you live."

Laura: "Yes. I'm glad you understand. I'm tired of people nagging me about my stuff."

As you can see, Ted didn't argue or push back. He simply rephrased, in his own words, what he heard his mother say to him. Through paraphrasing, Ted communicated to his mother that he was listening. This helped Laura feel more at ease and less defensive.

Clarifying: Even the best listener misses the mark from time to time. That's the benefit of paraphrasing: catching the error early. When your loved one tells you that you misunderstood or corrects you in some way, you shift to clarifying. Clarifying is all about asking questions to help you get it. Ask for the facts: who, what, when, where, why, and how; the more specific, the better. To tap into what might be going on under the specifics, ask feeling questions: "How did you feel about that?" or "What do you think about that?" Remember though, you're not interrogating your loved one or pressuring him to see things the way you do. Phrase your questions so that it's clear you're interested in understanding and helping your loved one, not in getting the upper hand. Let's see how Ted clarifies to keep the conversation with his mother on track:

Laura: "Yes, and I don't like people telling me what to do. Everyone wants me to throw away my stuff. That's what you want, isn't it? You want me to throw away all my stuff. Isn't that right?"

Ted: "So you think that I want you to throw away all your stuff. Is that right?"

Laura: "Yes. All you ever talk about is throwing away stuff."

Ted: "So, the way you see it is that all I want to do and talk about is throwing away your stuff. How does that make you feel?"

Laura: "How do you think it makes me feel? I feel like you don't really care about me. That's how I feel, as if you don't care about me. All you seem to care about is having me throw away my stuff."

Ted: "I'm sorry that you feel like I don't care about you."

Giving feedback: Feedback is your time to share calmly and without judgment your own thoughts, feelings, opinions, and desires with your loved one about what your loved one said. Good feedback is immediate. If you're upset by what your loved one said, it's not wise to stew too long before you tell him. Nor do you want to dilute the effect of your message by waiting too long to share. Good feedback is honest as well. An honest and direct message doesn't mean "brutal honesty" but that you explain to your loved one the effect of his message on you. For example, rather than "You're impossible to work with," you might say, "I'm feeling frustrated because you won't let me help." Ted has learned how to give his mother feedback in a caring and supportive way:

Laura: "Well, you can see why I think that. When you come to visit, you no sooner say hello than you are on me about getting rid of some stuff. You don't really care about me."

Ted: "I can see how you would feel like I don't care about you, but I want you to know that I do care. It's just that sometimes I come over, and it scares me to see you living in this house. That's when I start talking about throwing things away. In the past, I know I've told you to throw things away, but I do care and I want to help. I'm trying to be different with you. I want to try to help in a little different way."

Laura: "I know you do. I'm sorry, but sometimes I worry that you're going to start pushing me to throw things out the way you used to, that's all. I'm sorry."

Active Listening Role-Play

In this exercise, you'll practice active listening. With another family member, friend, or other team member, role-play a conversation. One of you will play the role of the "coach," and the other will play the role of the loved one with the hoarding problem. Include all the pieces of active listening (paraphrasing, clarifying, and giving feedback). Ask the person who plays the role of the family member to make it easy on you at first. Later, after you've had more practice at listening actively, the person playing your family member can turn up the heat a bit by becoming defensive or trying to argue with you. After each role-play, give each other feedback and try again until you feel confident that you can listen actively.

EMPATHIZING

Showing empathy toward your loved one doesn't mean that you agree with your loved one about everything, nor does it mean that you condone the way he lives. To show empathy is to show your loved one that you're trying to understand. Perhaps the best way to show empathy is through *reflective listening*, which involves reflecting back to your loved one with questions that show that you hear what he's thinking and feeling. Reflective listening is similar to active listening (which you learned earlier), in that you often paraphrase and clarify what your loved one says to you. However, in reflective listening, you emphasize understanding how your loved one *feels*, as well as what he thinks.

Ask questions that open conversations rather than close them down. Because we can only guess what someone's feeling, questions work best and, even if we guess wrong, show that we're trying. When you listen reflectively, you try to ask open-ended questions, questions that your loved one can't answer with a simple yes or no. Who, why, what, and how are great ways to phrase open-ended questions. For example, if you want to understand why it's very difficult for your loved one to discard a particular possession, you might ask, "Why do you like this so much?" If you want to understand why your loved one refuses help, you can try, "How do you feel about people helping you with the clutter?" or "What kind of help would be most useful to you?" By asking questions instead of commenting about what she says, you'll learn what's important to your loved one. This information may lead to new and perhaps more successful strategies to help her.

Summarize your understanding of what your loved one said. When your loved one answers your question, summarize what you thought you heard him say. This shows that you're listening. You might begin your summary by saying, "I want to make sure I'm hearing you right..." or "I think I heard you say..." In addition, check with your loved one that you correctly understood what she said: "I think I hear you saying that you're not ready for me to help you with the hoarding problem. Is that right?" Checking in like this tells your loved one that you're open to hearing whether you got something wrong.

Make statements or offer guesses about what your loved one is feeling. Empathy is about understanding how your loved one feels too. Because we can't know for certain what someone feels, we often have to guess, so ask your loved one if you understood correctly: "It looks as if you're feeling really anxious right now. Is that right?"

Make statements of praise. Don't forget to praise your loved one for his willingness to speak and work with you. In particular, any time your loved one is willing to discuss ways you can help, let him know that you appreciate his effort: "I know this is hard, but I really appreciate that you're talking to me. That really means a lot to me." This goes a long way toward opening doors to other conversations about how you might be able to help. Now, look at the way Ted shows empathy in his conversation with his mother, Laura.

> *Ted:* "You're going to handle the hoarding problem yourself. Do you have a plan?"

Laura: "Yes. I'll work on it a little bit every day. It's just hard to find the time to go through things, but I can do it. I just want to do it myself."

Ted: "It's important to you that you do this yourself without any help. Why is that?"

Laura: "Well, you and your sister think I can't take care of myself, but I can."

Ted: "You're an independent person, and you want us to remember that. Is that right?"

Laura: "Yes. You think I can't take care of myself. You think I don't know that all this clutter is a little dangerous. I do. You're just waiting to put me in an old people's home. I won't go."

Ted: "When we talk about helping you with the clutter, you worry that we're going to put you in a home and you'll lose your independence. You think our goal is to take away your independence, and that scares you. Is that right?"

Laura: "Yes. I've always been an independent person. You know that."

Ted: "Yes. We know that being independent is very important to you. We want you to live independently too. We really do."

Laura: "Good. I want to believe you. I do. It just scares me sometimes."

Giving Empathy Role-Play

In this exercise, you'll practice giving empathy to your loved one. With another family member, friend, or other team member, role-play a conversation. One of you will play the role of the "coach," and the other will play the role of the loved one with the hoarding problem. Follow all the guidelines for giving empathy (asking questions, summarizing your understanding, offering guesses, and praising). Ask the person who plays the role of the family member to make it easy on you at first. Later, after you've had more practice at giving empathy, the person playing your family member can turn up the heat a bit by becoming defensive or trying to argue with you. After each role-play, give each other feedback and try again until you feel confident that you can give empathy.

AGREEING

Now that you've listened to your loved one tell you how he feels and thinks about accepting help, and shown that you empathize, you've found some areas where the two of you agree and disagree. For example, Ted didn't agree with his mother that she could manage her hoarding problem on her own, without help from Ted or anyone, nor did he believe, as his mother did, that the hoarding problem was not so bad. However, Ted and his mother did agree that she was uncomfortable and, at times, risked slipping on the clutter. Ted could argue with his mother and try to convince her that his point of view is correct; however, he could also focus on the things they agree on and start there.

Find the common ground. Agreeing isn't just going along. Agreeing is a sincere and truthful statement that you and your loved one share some common ground. Therefore, the first step to agreeing is to find that common ground. Often, this is something that your loved one has already acknowledged or that you and your loved one agree on. Start there. Often, common ground is a goal or desire you share with your loved one, such as spending more time together as a family. In Ted's case, he shared his mother's wish for her to live independently. He could honestly say that if he were in his mother's shoes, he, too, would be worried that family members would ship him off to some assisted-living facility. When you acknowledge common ground, it's more likely that you'll be able to agree to work toward a common goal.

Do not argue or debate. Debating, arguing, or trying to make your point only leads to conflict, anger, and more hurt and resentment. This is particularly true when your loved one shares something that appears to be irrational: "If I throw something away, it will kill me." Your loved one believes what he believes, and although you don't have to confront him, you don't have to agree either. In these cases, change the subject or paraphrase: "Throwing something away is really hard for you."

Ask permission to share your opinion. When you see an opportunity to share your opinion, begin by asking permission from your loved one to share what you think or have observed. You might say, "Is it okay if I give you my take on this?" or "Would you like my opinion about this?" Your loved one may not agree with your opinion or follow your suggestion. However, you've likely shared your suggestions and opinions whether she wanted them or not, and she hasn't followed those either. At least, by asking permission you show respect and consideration even if she continues to disagree or disregard your opinions or suggestions. If she's going to disregard what you have to say, it's better that she at least experience you as caring and respectful.

Examine the advantages and disadvantages of accepting help. Rather than try to convince your loved one to accept help, take some time to explore with him the advantages and disadvantages of accepting help and not accepting help. There are pros and cons to both sides, and your loved one may be more open to accepting help if he feels that you and he have explored both sides of the issue in a collaborative and caring way.

Reflectively listen and highlight the advantages. Rather than disagree with the disadvantages of accepting help that your loved one identifies, respectfully pass over these and highlight the advantages of accepting help that arise: "Yes, that sounds like an important advantage." Without agreeing with the disadvantage, reflectively listen to communicate empathy: "You're worried that if you accept our help, we'll push you too fast. You see that as a disadvantage. Is that right?"

Correct misunderstandings. Don't agree when your loved one clearly misunderstands something about the problem of compulsive hoarding: "I hear you saying that you keep all these things because you lived through the Great Depression. The Depression doesn't cause hoarding problems. Many people lived through the Depression, and they don't have a hoard-ing problem." In addition, correct misunderstandings your loved one might have about the harm reduction approach and his role, your role, and the roles of other harm reduction team members. In addition, don't correct a misunderstanding by overstating or understating the facts, and don't lie. If you don't know the answer to the question, "Will the fire department really evict me?" tell your loved one that you're not certain but that you think it's possible—if it is.

Agree to disagree. You don't have to agree with everything your loved one says. For example, you may not be able to agree with your loved one's insistence that she's safe when you can see that she's not, or that it's not a big deal that she doesn't have running water or a functioning toilet. At these times, all you can do is agree to disagree. Calmly and in a caring way that shows respect for her viewpoint, say, "It looks as if we may have to agree to disagree on this one. I hope that's okay." Now, watch Ted weave these steps throughout his conversation with his mother:

> *Ted:* "So you want to work on the hoarding problem, but you don't want help from anyone. Is that right?
>
> *Laura:* "Yes. I can do it on my own. I can."
>
> *Ted:* "It sounds like doing it on your own is really important to you. You've always been very independent, and I admire that about you. You know, I would feel the same way if I were in your shoes. I would want people to let me try to do this on my own."

Ted reflectively listens to his mother and then finds some common ground. That isn't difficult for Ted, because he has always been a very independent person himself. Laura relaxes a little.

> *Laura:* "Yes. You and I are like that. We're very independent."
>
> *Ted:* "Yes, we are. I know that you want to do this on your own. I'm concerned though. May I tell you why?"
>
> *Laura:* "Yes, but I know what you're going to say. You think I can't do it."
>
> *Ted:* "Actually, you're a pretty determined lady. It just seems that it'll be very hard on you to try to do this all on your own. It's a tough decision to accept some help and give up a little independence rather than keep all your independence and do this big job on your own. Could we take a look at the advantages and disadvantages of this approach?"

Ted gets the problem out onto the table (doing it all without any help will be very hard on her) and then moves to talking with his mother about the advantages and disadvantages of doing it on her own, and the advantages and disadvantages of accepting some help with the hoarding problem.

Laura: "Yes. That's okay, but I have to tell you that it won't change my mind."

Ted: "Yes, I accept the possibility that it might not change your mind, but I appreciate that you're willing to talk to me about it. Now let's see. One advantage of managing the hoarding problem on your own is that you protect your independence. That's very important to you. What else?"

Laura: "Well, if I do it myself, I don't have to worry that you're going to throw something away."

Ted: "Yes. I can see why you're worried about that, but I agreed never to do that again, and you would be right there with me. I also promised I wouldn't touch anything without your permission. Remember? Haven't I done what I promised?"

Laura: "Yes. That's true."

Ted: "So, the advantages are that you maintain your independence, you aren't rushed, and you don't have to worry that I'm going to throw something away without your permission. Anything else?"

Laura: "No. Those are the main advantages."

Ted: "Okay. How about disadvantages?"

Laura: "Disadvantages. What do you mean?"

Ted: "Disadvantages to managing the hoarding problem all on your own, not accepting any help. Do you see any disadvantages?"

Laura: "Well. It's a big job. I guess it would be a lot of work."

Ted: "Yes, a lot of work. Is this how you want to spend all your time, clearing the clutter?"

Laura: "No. That's not how I want to spend my retirement years." [Laura laughs.]

Ted: "Right. That's no way to spend your retirement years. I agree. What else?"

Laura: "Well, I know that I'm going to need some help for a while. I've tried to manage the hoarding problem myself over the years, and I know it's not going to go away. I don't know if I can do this on my own year after year."

Ted: "Yes, I see it that way too. Managing the hoarding problem is a long-term job. Doing it on your own would be tough. Again, is that the way you want to spend your retirement years?"

Laura: "No, I guess not." [Laura laughs again.]

Ted: "Okay. Are there other disadvantages of trying to manage the hoarding problem without any help?"

Laura: "No. I think that's it."

Ted now summarizes and highlights the advantages of accepting help with the hoarding problem. Ted writes the advantages and disadvantages on a sheet of paper so that he and his mother can keep track of the conversation. Watch how he agrees and stresses the importance of the advantages that come to his mother if she decides to accept some help.

Ted: "So the first advantage of accepting some help with the hoarding problem is that you'll have more time to do fun things. I agree. You're retired, and you've worked hard. You deserve to have some fun. The second advantage is that you get support with the problem over time. You've seen that the problem doesn't go away and that it's tough to have to manage the problem on your own year after year. I agree. You've worked hard all your life; you deserve to rest and enjoy yourself. So, the main advantage of accepting some help is that you free up some time to enjoy your retirement years. Is that right?"

Laura: "Yes. I would like to enjoy these years more."

Ted: "Right. I would like that for you too. Now, let's look at the disadvantages of accepting some help. Do you see any disadvantages to accepting some help for the hoarding problem?"

Laura: "Disadvantages of accepting help—hmm. Well, I think we've already talked about those—you know, being rushed and scared you'd throw something out and losing my independence. That's it, I think."

Ted: "Yes. Those are all the disadvantages I can think of too. How about the advantages of accepting some help—the right kind of help, of course? Do you see any advantages to accepting some help for the hoarding problem?"

Laura: "Well, I guess if I let you and your sister help me, I'd get to see you two more often. I know it's hard on you to see my house, but I do miss you."

Ted: "Yes, we'd like to see you more often too, Mom. That would be a big advantage for me too. What else?"

Laura: "I can't think of anything else."

Ted: "I have an idea. Want to hear what it is?"

Laura: "Sure."

Ted: "Well, if we could straighten things a little better, we might be able to have Jamie's birthday here, like the old days. We used to have terrific birthday parties here. Remember?"

Laura: "Yes. I remember. I miss those too. That would be wonderful. Do you really think we could do that?"

Ted: "Well, I don't see why not. We'd just have to focus on a couple of places in the house, maybe the living room and the kitchen. We might be able to do that. What do you think?"

Laura: "That would be great."

Ted: "So, a major advantage of accepting help would be that we'd be able to have family gatherings at your place again, like in the old days. That would be great! What else?"

Laura: "Well, if I could move some stuff out of the kitchen, I could start to bake again. I miss that. Remember the great cakes I used to make?"

Ted: "Absolutely! If we could get the kitchen in shape, you could bake again. I know we would all love that. You're a great cook!"

The final step is to correct misunderstandings when they arise. You don't want to agree with your loved one just to agree. There'll be times when your loved one may not correctly understand what harm reduction means, what your role and his role might be if he accepts help, or what help would look like; or there may be misunderstandings about the hoarding problem itself. Correcting these misunderstandings in a calm and caring way averts incorrect expectations that may lead to conflict and resentment down the road.

Laura: "Well, if you'd lived through the Great Depression the way I did, you'd understand. That's why I don't like to throw things away."

Ted: "You see the Great Depression as causing the hoarding problem. May I give you my opinion on that?"

Laura: "Sure."

Ted: "I'm certain it was tough living through the Great Depression. I can't really imagine how hard that was on you, and I agree that it might make it a little more difficult for you to throw things out, but I don't think it explains the whole problem. Aunt Grace, your sister, grew up during the Great Depression and in the same house as you. She can throw things away. I don't think the Great Depression alone explains the hoarding problem."

Laura: "Well, Grace and I are different people. The Depression was harder on me, and that's the way I see it."

Ted: "Yes, you and Grace are different. The Depression was hard on you, and it's amazing how much you've accomplished in your life, given what you've been through over the years. I guess we're going to agree to disagree on this one. I hope that's okay. We don't have to agree on everything, do we?"

Laura: "No, we don't have to agree on everything. That's right."

PARTNERING

The truth of the matter is that your loved one is an adult. As an adult, he has the right to make his own decisions. As an adult, he doesn't like for people to tell him what to do, even if it's for his own good. As an adult, he doesn't have to listen to you if he doesn't want to listen. As an adult, he has the right to refuse help until legal authorities decide otherwise. Ted learned this lesson repeatedly when he rushed in to help his mother. Each time he pushed his mother to accept help, she pushed back to remind Ted that she was still his mother and that she could and would make her own decisions. Ted couldn't help his mother because she didn't see him as a partner who wanted to work with her. She saw him as someone who wanted to tell her what to do.

Listening, empathizing, and agreeing with his mother set the stage for Ted to partner with her, which is the final step in helping your loved one accept help. Ted introduced the idea of harm reduction and the goal of keeping certain areas in her home clear of clutter to make her safe and comfortable, rather than just clear out all her things. Laura was willing to accept help with that goal in mind. They forged a partnership and successfully negotiated the terms of that partnership. Ted knew that the partnership was fragile and that there would be many ups and downs, but he and his sister were prepared for that. They were in it for the long haul.

Over time, Ted noticed that his mother's mood had improved. She appeared to be less down and more open to accepting help from him and the other members of the harm reduction team. When he asked her about this, she said that she felt better because she was arguing less with Ted and his sister. Ted agreed with his mother. The arguing and conflict had certainly brought everyone down, but he thought there might be other reasons his mother was a bit more open to accepting help. He could see that she was less anxious and guarded with him and other people who came into her home to help. In part, this was because she had seen that Ted and the other team members had honored their part of the partnership. They didn't touch Laura's possessions without permission. They worked only on the harm reduction targets. They didn't argue or tell her what to do. In addition, Laura's insight into the hoarding problem improved a bit as she made progress in managing the hoarding problem. We've seen this happen with many of our clients with hoarding problems. As they dig out, their perspective on the clutter changes a bit, and they more readily acknowledge the many problems that go along with saving too much stuff.

L.E.A.P. Role-Play

In this exercise, you'll apply L.E.A.P. to helping your loved one accept help. With another family member, friend, or other team member, role-play a conversation. One of you will play the role of the "coach," and the other will play the role of the loved one with the hoarding problem. Include all the pieces of L.E.A.P. and practice "agreeing to disagree" about certain things. Ask the person who plays the role of the family member to make it easy on you at first. Later, after you've had more practice using L.E.A.P., the person playing your family member can turn up the heat a bit by becoming defensive or trying to argue with you. After each role-play, give each other feedback and try again. Continue the role-plays until you feel confident that you can use L.E.A.P. effectively to help your loved one accept help and to engage and reengage in the harm reduction process.

Assertiveness

We encourage you to set limits regarding what you will and won't tolerate when it comes to hoarding and clutter. This is particularly true if you live with someone who hoards. Through assertiveness, you communicate to your loved one the consequences his hoarding behavior has on you and your relationship with him. Sometimes, assertiveness can encourage your loved one to accept help or get the harm reduction plan back on track. Assertive statements communicate what you want (or don't want) to happen and what will happen if your loved one doesn't comply. It's essential that you communicate clearly and calmly. Keep your assertive statements brief, and, above all, don't argue. An assertive statement includes three parts.

Tell your loved one how you see things. Be as specific as you can when you tell your loved one how you see things and how you feel about it; for example, "Mom, you put a pile of newspapers on my bed. I'm very upset" or "Mom, I brought the kids over for a visit, but the front door's blocked again. I can't leave the kids here if I don't feel that they're safe."

Tell your loved one what you want. Even when your loved one is willing to comply with your request, she may have trouble doing this if she's not clear about what you want. Think about what you want, and then state it simply and directly, again, in as neutral and unemotional a way as possible; for example, "I want to feel that my kids are safe when they visit you."

State what you will or won't do if your loved one doesn't do what you ask. Stating a deadline by which there will be negative consequences may create the necessary push for your loved one to accept help from you or others. You can warn your loved one if it looks as if he's not following through, but try to be as neutral and matter-of-fact as you can; for example, "We agreed that you wouldn't store things in my room, and you broke your agreement. Please remove the newspapers from my bed before nine tonight or I'll move them into your room." Alternatively, you might say, "I'll ask the kids to play outside for a while until you and I clear away this stuff. If we can't clear away the stuff, I'll take the kids home." If your loved one fails to do what you ask her to do, don't be mean or spiteful. Just do what you said you would do without comment or fanfare. Your loved one will likely be upset with you when you follow through with the consequence, so stay calm and, above all, follow through.

Introducing Your Loved One to the Harm Reduction Approach

As you work to help your loved one accept help, many opportunities will arise to introduce the topic of harm reduction. In this chapter, you've learned how to increase the likelihood that your loved one will accept the harm reduction approach. Once your loved one is open to hearing about harm reduction, there are several ways to explain it to him. You can do this one on one or as a family. We recommend beginning by stating what you've observed and why you're concerned about the hoarding problem. If you're meeting as a family, each family member will share his or her observations and concerns. Remember to share your observations and concerns with care and respect. Even after you've set the stage, you can expect your loved one to respond with some anger and resentment. Use the listening and empathizing skills you've learned to keep the conversation on track. After you've shared your observations and concerns, state that you're sorry that the ways you've tried to help in the past weren't helpful or even welcome and that you're going to try to help in a different way this time, if your loved one permits you.

Next, explain how harm reduction differs from what your loved one may have tried in the past. As you explain harm reduction, emphasize that harm reduction focuses on the goal of keeping your loved one safe and comfortable by managing the hoarding problem rather than throwing all, or even a lot of, her things away. You can expect your loved one to have many questions about harm reduction. In particular, she'll want to know whether she'll have to discard possessions. Answer her questions directly and truthfully by saying that, at times, to keep her safe, you and she may have to discard some possessions, but the goal is not to discard more than is necessary to keep her safe and comfortable in her home. Give your loved one an idea of what that might look like: "For example, if we agreed to keep newspapers away from the stove, you and I might decide to recycle those newspapers, move them somewhere else, or throw them away. We'll work that out together."

Visualization

Managing a hoarding problem over the long term means that you're in for some ups and downs. To help you and your loved one get through the downs, it's important that you both have clear visions of why you're working together on this difficult problem. In this exercise, we would like for you and your loved one to take a few minutes to visualize what your loved one's life and home might look like once you're working effectively to manage the hoarding problem. Although you can imagine less-cluttered living spaces, we would like for you to visualize your loved one and you using those spaces in a way that enhances your relationship and family connections. For example, visualize a birthday party for a niece or grandson, or a family Thanksgiving celebration at the dining table. Visualize fun activities and good times. Alternatively, visualize the two of you just sitting together in a decluttered room, talking together about something other than the clutter. On a piece of paper, write your thoughts and feelings. Remember though, don't use this to make a point about whether it's important to accept help for the hoarding problem. It's an exercise to inspire hope and clarify your reasons for working together.

In this chapter, you learned several ways to help your loved one accept help. We emphasized listening skills and introduced L.E.A.P., a strategy that you'll use throughout the process of helping your loved one manage his hoarding problem. In addition, you learned how to use assertiveness to encourage your loved one to accept help, as well as set boundaries about the hoarding problem itself. Finally, you learned how to introduce your loved one to harm reduction as an alternative approach to managing his hoarding problem. The following chapter describes how to evaluate your loved one's harm potential and to begin the process of developing a harm reduction plan to manage his hoarding problem.

CHAPTER 5

Assessing Harm Potential

At an alarming rate, Lily has filled her apartment with bags of plastic bottles, newspapers, clothing, and knick-knacks that she bought at garage sales in the neighborhood. Although she uses a walker to get around in her apartment, last month she tripped over some clutter and broke her wrist. Her daughter, Sarah, has arranged to take turns with her three sisters in stopping by to check on their mother, and several of Lily's old bridge friends stop by from time to time too. Still, Sarah worries. Her mother's sight is poor, and she often can't find her heart medications in the paper-filled kitchen. Over the last year, Lily has developed diabetes, which has made her balance worse.

In another neighborhood, Sam is visiting his father, Harry, who lives alone in the home in which Sam and his brother were raised. Because of neglect, the house is falling down around Harry. The roof is dilapidated and leaks. The toilet and shower no longer work. Because Harry no longer has electrical power to his home, he uses candles for light and cooks his meals on a propane gas grill he keeps on the back porch. During the winter, Harry wheels the gas grill into the back of the family room and cooks there. Harry uses a five-gallon plastic bucket for a toilet and seldom bathes. Sam has tried to get Harry to move or at least to permit him to bring someone over to repair the house, but Harry refuses. Harry speaks to Sam and no one else.

As Lily's and Harry's situations illustrate, no two hoarding situations are the same, which means that every harm reduction plan is slightly different, because different hoarding situations have different levels of harm potential. Although Sarah is right to be concerned, her mother's harm potential is lower than Harry's, in part because she's open to having people enter her home, she appears willing to accept some help, and the sole current risk is that she'll slip and fall. Harry's harm potential, on the other hand, is much higher. He's isolated, and he won't permit others to enter his home. His home is dilapidated and trash-filled, and he uses candles to light it. In the winter, he uses a gas grill inside to cook his meals. He suffers with respiratory illness that's aggravated by the dust and mildew in the home, and he's not taking care of his most basic needs for hygiene and comfort. For these reasons, Harry's harm potential is higher.

Because harm reduction focuses on managing the potential harm your loved one faces each day she lives with her hoarding problem, the first step in creating a harm reduction plan is to assess your loved one's current harm potential. In this chapter, we begin by describing how to conduct a home assessment of your loved one's harm potential, and then move to describing the various harm potential factors that may influence, up or down, the risk your loved one faces from the hoarding problem. We present these factors in order of importance, beginning with safety. However, there's considerable overlap among these factors, because subtle changes in one factor can greatly influence another.

Conducting the Home Assessment

The home assessment should take one to two hours. For some people who hoard, especially if they're older, two hours may be a long time to concentrate and stay engaged in the assessment. If you anticipate that you or your loved one will need shorter visits, plan accordingly. You could schedule three briefer meetings that last forty-five minutes as a way to keep the energy up each time.

We recommend that only one family member or team member conduct the home assessment. These first visits are very difficult for people who hoard, and the more people there are walking around your loved one's home, the more frightened your loved one will feel. However, if others, such as the landlord or fire inspector, know about the hoarding problem, these people may insist that they be there too. We recommend meeting with the authorities ahead of the home visit to work out details, such as who'll speak to your loved one and who'll observe, to outline the conditions of the visit (no touching without permission), and to clarify and agree upon the goals of the home harm potential assessment. If your loved one is open to having several family members visit for the home assessment, we recommend that you invite those family members who'll be most involved in managing the hoarding problem over time, particularly family members with whom your loved one is on the best terms. Follow these guidelines when conducting your first home harm potential assessment:

Show respect. Don't react with shock or dismay to the conditions of the home. Remain neutral and matter of fact. Remember, your loved one is watching, and how you handle this initial visit can set the tone for future home visits. To put your loved one at ease, chat with her while you walk through the home. Show respect and ask your loved one for permission before you enter a room or open a closed door or cabinet, or even before touching a possession.

Be prepared. You may not be able to sit down or move around easily in the home. You may not be able to use the toilet there or get a drink of water. Anticipate these difficulties and plan accordingly. Consider how you might need to protect yourself during a home visit. Will you need to wear gloves, protective clothing, or a breathing mask? If you plan to wear protective clothing, discuss this with your loved one first. You might consider having hand wipes available in the car for afterward.

Explain the goal of the assessment. Before you begin to explore the home, explain the goal of the home assessment, which is to assess your loved one's level of harm potential; to identify harm reduction targets (for example, the staircase, the front door, the stove top), including areas of the home to be repaired; and to photograph each room and each potential harm reduction target.

Photograph potential harm reduction targets. Take photographs of each potential harm reduction target. If your loved one permits, take photographs of each room too, but the harm reduction targets are the most important. Photograph the harm reduction targets from most to least harm potential, because you'll want to make certain you get photographs of the most important harm reduction targets in case you run out of time.

L.E.A.P. to answer questions. During the home harm potential assessment, your loved one will likely have many questions. Try to answer them directly and truthfully. In fact, likely the first question your loved one will ask (and ask repeatedly) is whether you'll be discarding any of his possessions. We recommend that you remind your loved one that the goal of harm reduction is to manage the hoarding problem so that he's safe and comfortable. De-emphasize discarding and use L.E.A.P. (listen, empathize, agree, and partner; see chapter 4) to keep these conversations on track.

Complete the Harm Potential Assessment Form. This form (found later in this chapter) has sections for rating the severity of the hoarding problem and focuses on factors that increase or decrease your loved one's harm potential. To engage your loved one in the harm potential assessment, encourage her to complete her own harm potential assessment form. Her ratings relative to your ratings can give you more information about her level of insight and motivation about the hoarding problem.

Leave time to chat. Near the end of the home assessment, perhaps for ten minutes or so, chat with your loved one. Don't discuss the hoarding problem, and avoid other topics that you know are areas of past conflict and disagreement. Instead, chat with your loved one about what he has been doing, tell him about your children, or discuss topics that are of mutual interest. If your loved one has questions about the home assessment, answer his questions as best you can, but even then, try to end the visit with a friendly chat that strengthens your relationship.

If you accomplish nothing else during that first visit (say you forget your camera or leave the harm potential assessment form at home), we encourage you to make certain that you've left the door open for the next one. If you're respectful and patient, and have demonstrated that you're open and willing to meet your loved one halfway, then you've done well.

Safety

By safety, we mean any situation within your loved one's home that puts her at risk of death or physical injury. Injury or death by fire or by tripping and falling are the most common risks that people who hoard face. Cluttered stairways are another unsafe situation, as are doorways that your loved one has blocked with piles of newspapers or possessions so that she can't exit her home quickly in case of a fire or earthquake.

We've adapted and expanded the Activities of Daily Living for Hoarding (ADL-H) (Steketee and Frost 2007) to assess the harm potential for your loved one. The Harm Potential Assessment Form identifies particular conditions of the living situation that may affect your loved one's safety and health, as well as the degree to which the clutter interferes with your loved one's ability to complete ordinary activities like bathing, dressing, and preparing meals.

Although we've organized the Harm Potential Assessment Form to emphasize safety over health and comfort, we recognize that there's considerable overlap among all these factors. If your loved one is frail, what affects his health can affect his safety. For example, if the living situation is safe (your loved one is safe from injury or fall) but uncomfortable, he may be less safe if he is frail or has a medical condition that can be worsened by an uncomfortable living situation (such as respiratory illness or cardiac disease).

Harm Potential Assessment Form

Conditions of the Living Situation That Affect Safety

This part of the form focuses on assessing the degree to which your loved one's home is unsafe. Please rate the degree to which each item on the following list concerns you by marking it with a number between 1 and 5 (where 1 is no concern and 5 is severe concern).

Problems Affecting Safety in the Home	Degree of Concern (1–5)
1. Parts of the home pose a fire hazard (for example, stove covered with paper, flammable material near the furnace, or flammable solvents stored in the home).	
2. Parts of the home are unsanitary (for example, buckets filled with urine or feces, other areas of home soiled with urine or feces, strong odor, or bathrooms unclean or unusable).	
3. Medical emergency personnel would have difficulty entering or moving equipment through the home.	
4. Exits (doors) from the home are blocked.	
5. Windows are blocked.	

6. It's unsafe to move up or down the stairs, or along other walkways.	
7. There's clutter on the floor that obstructs pathways.	
8. Heavy items are stacked high.	
9. Glass or sharp items are stacked high.	
10. There are frayed or exposed electrical cords.	
11. Smoke alarms are absent or don't work.	
12. There's pooled water in the home that's not contained.	
13. There's structural damage to the floors of the home.	
14. There's structural damage to the walls or beams of the home.	
15. There's structural damage to the ceilings of the home.	
16. There's structural damage to the stairs in the home.	

Conditions of Living Situation That Affect Health and Comfort

This part of the form focuses on the condition of your loved one's living situation that may affect her health and comfort. Mark a number between 1 and 5 (where 1 is no concern and 5 is severe concern) that best indicates how much the conditions in the home may affect your loved one's health and comfort.

Problems Affecting Health in the Home	Degree of Concern (1–5)
17. Structural damage (such as rotted floors, wet walls, and dilapidated roof).	
18. Rotten food is in the home or refrigerator.	
19. Home infested with insects.	
20. Home infested with rodents.	
21. Dead animals (rodents or pets) are in the home.	
22. Human urine or feces are in the home.	
23. Animal feces or urine is in the home.	
24. Blood is in the home.	
25. Vomit is in the home.	
26. Mold, mildew, or fungus is in the home.	
27. Water is turned off or not working.	
28. Heat is turned off or not working.	
29. Electricity is turned off or not working.	
30. Trash (garbage collection) service has ceased.	

Activities Affected by Clutter or Hoarding Problem

Sometimes clutter in the home can prevent your loved one from doing ordinary activities, such as bathing or preparing meals. For each of the following activities, mark a number between 1 and 5 (where 1 means "can do easily" and 5 means "unable to do") that best indicates how much difficulty you believe your loved one has with doing this activity because of the clutter or hoarding problem. If your loved one has difficulty doing the activity because of medical or physical limitations (for example, your loved one is unable to bend or move quickly because of a stroke or balance problems), don't include this in your rating. If the situation isn't relevant to your loved one's situation (for example, your loved one doesn't have pets or the living situation doesn't include a kitchen), mark "NA" (not applicable).

Activity	Ability to Perform Activity (1–5 or NA)
31. Prepare food.	
32. Use the refrigerator.	
33. Use the stove.	
34. Use the kitchen sink.	
35. Eat at the table.	
36. Move around inside the house.	
37. Exit the home quickly.	
38. Use the toilet.	
39. Use the bath or shower.	
40. Use the bathroom sink.	
41. Answer the door quickly.	
42. Sit on the sofa or in a chair.	
43. Sleep in bed.	
44. Do laundry.	
45. Find important things (such as bills, tax forms, and medications).	
46. Care for animals.	

Adapted and expanded from *Compulsive Hoarding and Acquiring: Workbook*, Gail Steketee and Randy O. Frost, eds., 206–07 (New York: Oxford University Press, Inc., 2007). Used by permission of Oxford University Press, Inc.

Comfort

At times, people who hoard are surprisingly unconcerned about their comfort. Your loved one may tell you that it doesn't bother him that he sleeps on a sliver of his bed or that he must stand to eat his meals. However, more often, people who hoard ask you to help them live more comfortably in an unsafe home. At these times, wanting to live more comfortably can motivate them to work with you to improve their safety as well, particularly when you help them see that comfort and safety are often related. However, don't get caught up in working to improve comfort at the expense of improving the safety of the living situation. Safety always trumps comfort. Remind your loved one that if you and he don't make it safer for him to live in his home, he may not be able to live there at all—comfortably or not.

Support

Many people with a hoarding problem are quite isolated, and some of them prefer it that way. Your loved one may tell you that she prefers hanging out with her possessions to hanging out with you or her friends. However, the more isolated your loved one is, the more likely that harm will come to her, because if for no other reason, no one is checking on her to see that she's okay. For example, Harry's harm potential is greater than Lily's, because Lily is less isolated and more open to having people enter her home, and has a larger group of friends and family members.

Family support is perhaps the most important form of social support, because family members are likely to be the most involved over time in managing a harm reduction plan. For that reason, it's essential that you improve your relationship with your loved one as much as possible. As a rule, the better your family functions, the more likely that harm reduction will succeed.

However, family members aren't necessarily the only source of support for your family member. Anyone who drops by regularly as part of her professional role can help, even if she serves only as another set of eyes to monitor your loved one's safety and comfort. In addition, you can take advantage of the "visitor effect," whereby your loved one works to clear the clutter because someone's dropping by to visit. The bottom line is this: the lower your loved one's level of social support, the higher his harm potential. Use the following form to assess how much support your loved one currently has.

Assessing Level of Support

If you know the answers to these questions, complete this part of the assessment yourself. If you don't know, ask your loved one or other family members. For each of the following questions, please mark the answer that best approximates what you know or what your loved one tells you. If the question isn't relevant to your loved one's situation (for example, your loved one isn't employed), mark "NA."

Answer Key for Top Portion of Table:

O = Often (1 to 3 times per week)

S = Sometimes (1 or more times per month)

N = Never

NA = Not applicable

Answer Key for Lower Portion of Table:

Y = Yes

N = No

M = Maybe

NA = Not applicable

Question	Answer (O, S, N, or NA)
1. How often does your loved one see coworkers?	
2. How often does your loved one see her spouse, partner, or significant other?	
3. How often does your loved one speak to his siblings, parents, children, or grandchildren?	
4. How often does your loved one speak to, or do something with, a friend?	
5. How often does your loved one attend church, synagogue, or mosque?	

Question	Answer (O, S, N, or NA)
6. How often does your loved one meet regularly with a therapist, counselor, psychologist, or psychiatrist?	
7. How often do people who provide support services (visiting nurses, meal delivery services) come to your loved one's home?	
8. How often does your loved one attend service club meetings or organized groups (for example, a book club or walking group)?	
9. How often does your loved one speak to neighbors?	
10. How often does your loved one invite others to participate in activities (outside her home)?	
11. How often does your loved one accept invitations from *you or other family members* to do things together?	
12. How often does your loved one call *you or another family member* to go to a movie or concert, or to do something else fun together?	
13. How often does your loved one call a *friend* to go to a movie or concert, or to do something else fun together?	
14. How often does your loved one call a *friend* for support and comfort?	
15. How often does your loved one call *you or another family member* for support and comfort?	
16. How often does your loved one make an effort to keep in touch with old friends?	

Question	Answer (Y, N, M, or NA)
17. Does your loved one know the names of his neighbors and anything about them (such as what they do, or the names and ages of their children)?	
18. Is your loved one on good terms with her physician?	
19. Does your loved one have difficulty making new friends?	
20. Does someone visit your loved one to help him store, organize, or get rid of things?	

Insight and Motivation

In general, the less insight your loved one has about his hoarding problem, the less likely that he'll accept help and agree to work with you. For this reason, the lower your loved one's insight about his hoarding problem, the higher his harm potential. You may find it helpful to ask questions that try to get at whether your loved one sees the potential risk of a situation in the same way you do. For example, you might point to a pile of newspapers near the top of the stove and ask your loved one, "Have you tried to keep this area clear?" If he answers no, this suggests that he doesn't see the situation as dangerous. If he answers yes, ask him why. If he sees the danger in this situation, he might say, "Because I worry that some of the newspapers will fall onto the stove top when I'm cooking." Take care not to say, "Do you see that this situation is dangerous?" or "Tell me why these newspapers shouldn't be here." This sounds accusatory, and your loved one may not answer you. In addition to putting your loved one on the defensive, you don't find out whether he sees the situation as dangerous. Use the following form to assess your loved one's level of insight and motivation.

Assessing Insight and Motivation

Following is a list of a few factors that may influence your loved one's level of motivation. For each of the following questions, please fill in the answer that best approximates what you know or what your loved one tells you.

Answer Key:

N = Not (0–25 percent)

L = A little (26–50 percent)

V = Very (51–75 percent)

X = Extremely (76–100 percent)

Question	Answer (N, L, V, X)
1. How motivated is your loved one to work with you on a harm reduction plan?	
2. How open is your loved one to having people come into the home to work on a harm reduction plan?	
3. How open is your loved one to accepting other forms of help, such as medication (if that would lessen his fatigue or make it easier for him to focus)?	
4. How open is your loved one to having people enter the home to repair broken appliances or anything else that needs repair?	
5. How close are you and your loved one to seeing eye-to-eye regarding which situations are dangerous?	

Other Factors

Any number of other factors can increase your loved one's harm potential. If your loved one has another psychological or psychiatric condition (in addition to the hoarding problem), she may have greater difficulty following through with her harm reduction plan, thereby increasing her harm potential. For example, if your loved one feels severely and chronically depressed, she may fatigue easily and have trouble concentrating, which makes it difficult for her to work effectively with you when clearing the harm reduction targets, even when she wants to work. Many people who hoard also suffer from social phobia (social anxiety disorder). If she's extremely shy and avoids interacting with people, she may be reluctant to let people into her home or to work with people whom she doesn't know well on the harm reduction team.

If your loved one has significant alcohol or drug problems, his harm potential is greater, in part because he may be less open to help out of fear that family members will discover his alcohol or substance use. If he's often under the influence of alcohol or drugs, he may not be able to work with you effectively. In addition, if your loved one smokes and does so inside his home, his harm potential is greater because of the fire risk.

If your loved one has a current or chronic medical condition, her harm potential may be greater. For example, a hoarding problem can worsen some medical conditions, such as asthma, allergies, emphysema, or other respiratory problems. If your loved one has a life-threatening illness, such as a heart condition, the hoarding situation may make it difficult for medical emergency personnel to reach her if she needs help immediately, which thereby increases her harm potential. If your loved one is taking medications for a medical problem, these medications may cause her to fatigue easily, affect her memory, or lessen her motivation to work on the hoarding problem.

If your loved one has physical limitations, these may increase his harm potential. This is particularly true for older adults who may use walkers, canes, wheelchairs, or crutches to move around their homes, or who have balance and gait problems. Sensory limitations, such as poor vision or hearing, can make it difficult for your loved one to work with you on a harm reduction plan. If he can't hear what you're saying or see what you're pointing to, he may have trouble keeping up with you as you clear harm reduction targets. In addition, poor vision increases the likelihood that he may slip and fall in his cluttered home, thereby amplifying his harm potential.

Any of these factors increases your loved one's harm potential, and it's essential that your loved one's harm reduction program include some plan to help her with these. Use the following worksheet to assess for other conditions that may also affect your loved one's harm potential.

Assessing Other Conditions

Any number of factors can increase your loved one's harm potential. Look at the following list and, in a notebook or on a sheet of paper, write down and describe all the medical, physical, sensory, and psychological conditions that might influence your loved one's ability to participate in a harm reduction plan.

- Medical problems

- Physical limitations

- Sensory limitations

- Other psychiatric or psychological conditions (for example, depression, ADHD, social phobia, OCD, bipolar disorder)

- Other factors

Acquisition Pathways

Not everyone with a hoarding problem compulsively acquires things, but most do. An effective harm reduction plan identifies the multiple ways your loved one brings items into his home and includes strategies for closing these doors. For example, if your loved one acquires newspapers and catalogs through the mail, you might include in his harm reduction plan a way to decrease this flow, such as working with him to remove his name from catalog mailing lists or encouraging him to switch to online versions of his favorite newspapers. In the appendix, we describe how you can go about removing your loved one from mailing lists.

The greater the flow of possessions into your loved one's home, the greater her harm potential, if for no other reason than that it's difficult for you and the other members of the harm reduction team to keep up with the relentless flow. Use the following worksheet to determine what methods of acquisition are most common and problematic for your loved one.

Assessing Acquisition Factors

The greater the flow of possessions into your loved one's home, the greater his harm potential. Look at the following list and, in a notebook or on a sheet of paper, write down and describe the particular ways possessions enter your loved one's home.

- Through the mail (catalogs, junk mail, newspapers, magazines, periodicals)

- Through free samples (salt or pepper packets, paper napkins, free newspapers, handbills)

- Through purchasing (garage, tag, or yard sales; big-box stores; thrift stores; sales; Internet shopping; TV shopping)

- Through searching through trash (in trash bins or Dumpsters and set-asides for bulk pick-up days)

- Through the routine efforts of others (friends sending articles, relatives giving gift subscriptions to magazines, people bringing free things or extras, holiday gifts)

- Through family inheritances (receiving furniture and china when a relative passes away)

- Through borrowing (libraries, tool share programs)

- Through stealing or shoplifting

- Through neighborhood foraging (picking things up off the street or on the side of the road)

Identifying Harm Reduction Targets

An effective harm reduction plan begins with a comprehensive assessment of all the factors that may increase or decrease your loved one's harm potential. You and other harm reduction team members will focus directly on these factors, which we call "harm reduction targets." A harm reduction target may include an area in the home that you and your loved one agree to keep clear, such as around the stove or furnace. Other harm reduction targets may include working to decrease (at least partially) the flow of things into your loved one's home. Arranging for the safe storage of important documents or electronic payment of routine bills can be harm reduction targets too, as can arranging for routine medical exams or home-delivered meals.

Look at the Harm Reduction Planning Worksheet below. We've listed typical harm reduction targets and left space for you to identify those that are unique to your loved one. Remember that many factors can influence your loved one's harm potential, so don't overlook targets that you think aren't big-ticket problems. We ask you to rate the risk (and comfort) on a 0 to 10 scale so that you can keep your eye on the high-risk (and therefore high-priority) targets. However, sometimes what appears at first to look like a low-risk problem (gas grill on the porch) can become a high-risk situation (gas grill brought inside during the winter).

Harm Reduction Planning Worksheet

Safety Targets

Refer to the Harm Potential Assessment Form (introduced earlier) to review what hazards exist in your loved one's home. Choose targets based on those items that you rated as severe threats. On the following lines, describe and rate the safety risk level (0 to 10, where 10 is "extreme risk") of each harm reduction target. Try not to give targets the same safety risk number. If you estimate three targets at a safety risk of 9, rate them 9.2, 9.4, or 9.6 to clarify the priority.

Safety Target	Risk (0 to 10)

Safety Target	Risk (0 to 10)

Health Targets

On the following lines, describe and rate the health risk level (0 to 10, where 10 is "extreme risk") of each harm reduction target. Try not to give targets the same health risk number. If you estimate three targets at a health risk of 9, rate them 9.2, 9.4, or 9.6 to clarify the priority.

Health Target	Risk (0 to 10)

Comfort Targets

On the following lines, describe and rate the discomfort level (0 to 10, where 10 is "extreme discomfort") of each harm reduction target. Try not to give targets the same discomfort level number. If you estimate three targets at a discomfort level of 9, rate them 9.2, 9.4, or 9.6 to clarify the priority.

Comfort Target	Discomfort (0 to 10)

Medical, Physical, Memory, and Sensory Limitation Targets

On the following lines, describe your loved one's medical, physical, memory, and sensory limitations. Estimate your loved one's risk (0 to 10, where 10 is "extreme risk") of living in the hoarding situation with this limitation. Try not to assign targets the same level of risk. If you estimate three targets at a health risk of 9, rate them 9.2, 9.4, or 9.6 to clarify the priority.

Medical, Physical, Memory, and Sensory Limitation Target	Risk (0 to 10)

Accommodation Targets

On the following lines, list potential accommodations that you may require to manage the hoarding problem. Rate each potential accommodation based on its importance (0 to 10, where 10 is "most important") in managing your loved one's hoarding problem. Try not to give targets the same importance level. If you estimate three targets at an accommodation importance level of 9, rate them 9.2, 9.4, or 9.6 to clarify the priority. Brainstorm with your loved one, other family members, or other harm reduction team members about what potential accommodations your loved one may require. Harm reduction team members, such as psychiatrists, visiting nurses, and professional organizers, can give you some ideas. Would a hearing aid help? Would it help to ask the food delivery service to place food on a washable dish and put plastic containers in the trash? Would it help to get your loved one off junk-mail lists or to divert mail delivery to a post office box?

Accommodation Target	Importance (0 to 10)

Financial Harm Targets

On the following lines, describe and rate the financial risk level (0 to 10, where 10 is "extreme risk") of each harm reduction target. Try not to give targets the same financial risk number. If you estimate three targets at a financial risk of 9, rate them 9.2, 9.4, or 9.6 to clarify the priority.

Financial Harm Target	Risk (0 to 10)

As you go through the Harm Reduction Planning Worksheet, you'll have many questions for your loved one. In fact, how your loved one answers questions about harm reduction targets can give you valuable information about the potential risk of a target. We mentioned how the way your loved one answers a question can suggest his level of insight into the potential danger of a situation. In addition, the reasons your loved one keeps something in one place rather than another can help you later generate alternative strategies for keeping the target area clear. How and why he uses something can help you understand when a situation may be dangerous and when it may not. For example, if your loved one tells you he sometimes prepares meals at home but you can see that he has cluttered the stove top, you might ask him how he cooks. He might tell you that sometimes he uses an electric hot plate that he sets atop the clutter on the counter or that he cooks outside on a gas grill (except in the winter when he brings the grill inside). We recommend that you ask the following questions to gather more information about potential harm reduction targets.

Identifying Harm Reduction Targets

1. How often do you cook meals on the stove?

2. How often do you sleep in your bed?

3. How often do you use the shower?

4. What makes getting around your home hard for you?

5. Do you lean on the piles of newspapers (or stuff) to steady yourself?

6. Do you use a cane or other device to get about, and does it help?

7. How often has the power company turned off the power? What did you use for light and heat?

8. How often do you miss paying a bill because you can't find your checkbook or because you've misplaced the bill?

9. What doesn't work in your home (refrigerator, stove, or toilet)? How do you cook your meals?

10. Where do you use the toilet?

11. How often do you forget to take your medications, and where do you keep them?

12. Do you ever misplace the medication bottles or prescriptions?

13. How often do you open the mail?

14. How often have you fallen in the home in the past year? Where in the home were you when you fell?

15. Have you ever received an eviction notice [if your loved one rents] or other correspondence from your landlord?

16. How often do you clean out spoiled contents from the refrigerator?

17. Is there anything I haven't asked about that you think may be a potential danger in your home?

In this chapter, you learned how to conduct a home assessment in order to gather the information you'll need to design a harm reduction plan for your loved one. In addition, you learned strategies for evaluating your loved one's harm potential that focus on her safety, comfort, level of support, and insight and motivation to work on the hoarding problem. Finally, you learned how to identify potential harm reduction targets that are the basis of your loved one's harm reduction plan. The following chapter describes how to take the information you've gathered and create a harm reduction plan to manage your loved one's hoarding problem.

CHAPTER 6

Creating a Harm Reduction Plan

By this point, you've set the stage for harm reduction by building trust and respect through showing that you care and understand. Using strategies like L.E.A.P, you've opened the door for your loved one to accept help from you and others. In this chapter, you'll learn how to create a harm reduction plan. You'll learn how to put together the harm reduction team and set realistic harm reduction goals. Once you've created the harm reduction plan, you'll learn how to formalize the harm reduction contract, which guides the harm reduction plan over time.

Features of a Harm Reduction Plan

All harm reduction plans share common features. First, an effective harm reduction plan includes a group of people dedicated to working with your loved one to manage her hoarding problem. Harm reduction team members (including your loved one) work together to set harm reduction goals and to overcome the many problems that arise when managing a hoarding situation over time. Second, an effective harm reduction plan includes clear, realistic, and measurable harm reduction goals and a method for monitoring progress toward those goals. Because harm reduction assumes that your loved one has little or no insight about the hoarding problem, it's essential that the harm reduction goals are realistic given the realities of most hoarding situations. Third, an effective harm reduction plan is flexible and includes any strategy that can help your loved one manage the hoarding problem. *Anything that helps* is the second anthem of harm reduction. You might work to get your loved one's name off junk-mail or direct-mail catalog lists. You might contact a plumber to come to your loved one's home and repair her shower and toilet. Your loved one's harm reduction plan may include a few strategies or many.

Last, an effective harm reduction plan includes a harm reduction contract that clearly spells out the harm reduction goals, targets, and agreements. Harm reduction contracts aren't set in stone. They're living documents that change as needed. A harm reduction contract formalizes the agreements you and your loved one make and is the focus for all future discussions about how well or poorly the harm reduction plan is working.

Putting the Harm Reduction Team Together

Putting the harm reduction team together is the first step in creating a harm reduction plan, and perhaps the most important. The harm reduction team will make many of the decisions that follow. Most likely, you, your loved one, and other family members will be the primary members of the harm reduction team. However, you may want to consider including professionals or other people with special expertise who might help.

Putting together an effective harm reduction team isn't as easy as it might sound. If you've had trouble organizing your family for a reunion or a holiday get-together, think about the trouble you may face as you try to organize a team to help your loved one. In fact, some family members have never had a good relationship with their loved one, and the hoarding problem has only made things worse.

Wanted: Effective Harm Reduction Team Members

Not everyone can be an effective harm reduction team member. There's no shame in this. The complexities of most hoarding problems challenge the patience and resourcefulness of even the most experienced mental health professionals. If you have serious doubts about whether you have what it takes to handle this difficult job, it's best to step aside and participate in other ways. As you put together a harm reduction team for your loved one, you're looking for people who have certain qualities.

Patience: An effective team member is patient. Hoarding tends to be a lifelong struggle for most people, particularly if they have little or no insight or motivation to accept help. As a team member, your goal is to help your loved one manage the hoarding problem as long as she's at risk. You might work with your loved one for ten or fifteen years on managing her hoarding problem. This takes patience—a lot of patience.

Stakeholding: An effective team member has a stake in the harm reduction process. An effective team member can tell you what's at stake for him. Your sister might tell you that she wants to worry less about your loved one. The landlord might tell you that he wants to be able to reassure the other tenants that they're safe from fire and rodent infestations. The visiting nurse might tell you that she wants to know that your loved one can find her medications or move around her apartment without falling. Having a stake in the harm reduction plan means that each stakeholder gets something too: less worry, less conflict, or the recognition that he or she is acting professionally and responsibly.

Time: An effective team member has the time for team meetings and home visits, and time to help in other ways. Time is a rare and precious commodity in today's world. You may have children and a family of your own. You may have a job, friends, and a million other things to do. Finding time to help your loved one won't be easy. Again, the more team members, the better, because people can share these responsibilities over time. Nevertheless, when a team member's turn comes, it's essential that he or she can make the time to help.

No current and ongoing conflicts: An effective team member won't have current and ongoing conflicts with your loved one. This isn't the same as never having a conflict with your loved one. You can expect team members and your loved one to disagree as they work together to manage the hoarding problem. However, if a team member has ongoing disagreements with your loved one about many things, including the harm reduction process, you may ask this person to help in other ways, such as by offering to make calls or dropping by for social visits. Later, as the frequency of conflicts with your loved one decreases, you might offer to let that person serve on the harm reduction team. For now, though, it's okay to wait.

Useful skills: An effective team member has some useful skills in addition to a strong back and patience. Perhaps you're good with your hands and can repair anything. Perhaps your brother has excellent negotiation skills, and your aunt is great at organizing. People who are good at problem solving are often invaluable members of a harm reduction team. You might have a plumber, counselor, or visiting nurse on the harm reduction team, each with skills that will help your loved one manage her hoarding problem. However, no matter how handy a team member, if she doesn't have the previously mentioned qualities—patience, a stake in the harm reduction process, time, and the ability to get along well with your loved one—she may not be a good candidate for the harm reduction team. Regardless of her skills, they don't do you much good if your loved one won't let her in the door.

When to Include Professionals on the Harm Reduction Team

Many times, it makes sense to include professionals on your loved one's harm reduction team. We use the term "professional" to mean anyone who has certain skills, who can provide specific services, or who has access to other resources and thereby can help you in some way to manage your loved one's hoarding problem. For example, if you or other family members aren't handy, you might want to include someone on the harm reduction team who is so that he can repair doors, toilets, showers, or anything else in disrepair. Having one person you can rely on to handle general repairs is better than parading a series of tradespeople through your loved one's home. These professionals don't have to attend every harm reduction team meeting, but if they're available and interested, it could be very helpful in developing their relationship with your loved one. Even after the person has repaired your loved one's home, you may need additional repairs later, and it would be much easier to bring back the same person whom your loved one knows and trusts.

If you aren't able to organize your loved one's possessions yourself, you may want to hire a professional organizer to help. Professional organizers teach strategies and set up systems that can help you and your loved one organize possessions and stay on top of the clutter. Other professionals, such as your loved one's therapist, counselor, or physician, can help you access other resources that might help your loved one manage her hoarding problem. Prescribing medications to help with your loved one's depression or inattention, arranging delivery of meals to your loved one, or simply agreeing to visit your loved one to monitor her safety and comfort can be enormously helpful.

When Professionals Insist on Joining the Harm Reduction Team

At times, you may not have a choice about whether to include a professional on the harm reduction team. The professional will insist on being involved. Generally, this occurs when a hoarding situation becomes public or when the situation is still private but a professional is concerned that it may need to become public if you and other family members can't quickly ensure that your loved one can live safely in his home.

If other people are involved or will soon become involved with your loved one's hoarding problem, we encourage you to ask them to join your loved one's harm reduction team. You can expect a great deal of resistance from your loved one, who may insist that she doesn't want to sit across the table from the person. You may need to use everything you learned previously (see chapter 4) to convince your loved one to work with the person. It's always better to have an ally than an adversary when it comes to managing a serious hoarding problem.

In addition, as we describe in chapter 8, the adult protective service worker, the fire chief, or the code enforcement officer can provide the needed pressure to convince your loved one to accept ongoing help with his hoarding problem. Many times, your loved one will be more open to working with the fire chief than with other professionals. He may accept that the fire chief's job is to protect his safety as well as that of the community. On the other hand, he may think the code enforcement officer's or adult protective services worker's job is to evict him.

Creating the Harm Reduction Plan

Now that you've put together your harm reduction team and completed a harm potential assessment for your loved one, it's time to create a harm reduction plan to manage the hoarding problem. An effective harm reduction plan includes four components: (1) realistic harm reduction goals; (2) a way to monitor progress toward the designated harm reduction goals; (3) a list of all the strategies that you and other harm reduction team members will use to help your loved one manage the hoarding problem; and (4) a harm reduction contract that clearly spells out the harm reduction goals, strategies, and agreements. In the next section, we describe each component of the harm reduction plan that you and your loved one will create.

Your Goals, My Goals, Our Goals

An effective harm reduction plan includes clearly identified and agreed upon harm reduction goals. Although you might think the goals of harm reduction are obvious, you may discover that many of the early harm reduction team meetings focus on identifying and negotiating which harm reduction goals are the most important. Of course, this begs the question, "Important to whom?"

Patricia has spoken to her seventy-seven-year-old mother, Margaret, about a harm reduction plan, and Margaret is guarded but open to the idea. Patricia put together her mother's harm reduction team, which includes herself and Margaret; Patricia's younger brother, Mark; Margaret's landlord; and Margaret's visiting nurse. Patricia opened the first meeting by asking each team member to state his or her goals for the harm reduction plan.

The landlord stated that his goal was to get the apartment clean as soon as possible and keep it that way. He said that other tenants were beginning to complain about the smell from Margaret's apartment and that he'd have to evict her if she didn't keep the apartment clean. The visiting nurse stated that her goal was to help Margaret manage her diabetes. She wanted Margaret to permit her to stop by every week so that she could check her blood sugar. In addition, because the diabetes had reduced the circulation to Margaret's feet and made it difficult for her to walk, she wanted to make certain that Margaret could move safely in her apartment.

Patricia looked at her brother, Mark, who said his goal was to make certain that his mother could go on living safely in her apartment. Patricia nodded and thought that Mark perhaps had another goal too. Patricia knew that Mark was in a panic about his mother's living situation. It was true that Mark loved his mother and worried about her. However, he also was desperate to keep his mother in the apartment. He knew that if the landlord evicted his mother, she would have to move in with him. He owned a large house that he and his wife shared, while Patricia lived in a one-bedroom apartment.

Margaret crossed her arms and stated that she didn't need help, and suspiciously looked at every member of the team. When Patricia pressed her mother to state her harm reduction goal, she said her goal was for everyone to leave her alone. Patricia was the last to speak. She said her goal was to worry less about her mother. She said that while she wanted her mother to live independently, she knew she might not be able to do that unless she and the others could help her manage the hoarding problem so that she was safe.

Harm reduction team members don't always come to the table with the same goals for your loved one. Team members have different roles, different responsibilities, and different interests. This is understandable and to be expected. However, it's essential that the harm reduction plan for your loved one include the goals of all team members. A team member's goal represents his or her stake in the harm reduction process. It's not necessary that harm reduction team members agree that every goal is a good goal. It's necessary, however, that they agree that the goal is important and thereby valid to a particular team member. For example, Mark's unspoken goal was to keep his mother in her apartment to avoid having to take her into his home. It's not helpful to judge Mark for this. Taking someone with a hoarding problem into your home can create any number of difficult problems. Patricia would try to validate for Mark the value of this goal so that he could be fully engaged in the harm reduction process.

In conclusion, you may come with one goal for your loved one, and others might come with different goals for your loved one. This is expected. Your job is to work with the team to create common goals that everyone on the team can support. This isn't an easy task, but it's doable. In fact, the act of creating shared goals can help all team members feel that they're part of the solution to the hoarding problem and help them buy into the harm reduction plan.

Agree to Realistic Harm Reduction Goals

As we described, a realistic harm reduction goal is a shared goal. However, realistic harm reduction goals have other important features. Realistic harm reduction goals are (1) concrete and specific, (2) doable, (3) can be quickly monitored and measured in some way, and (4) focus on safety first. In addition, most harm reduction goals include a harm reduction target. As mentioned, typically targets identify areas to keep clear of clutter but also can include the ways possessions come into your loved one's home (acquiring at garage sales or through delivery of junk mail or newspapers), as well as other problems or factors (other psychological or medical problems) that might increase or decrease your loved one's harm potential. Therefore, when you create a harm reduction goal, you first identify a target and then describe what you want to achieve toward that target. For example, keep an area clear of clutter, take the kitchen garbage out once each day, and recycle all newspapers each week are examples of harm reduction goals. In this section, we describe these four important features of realistic harm reduction goals.

Concrete and specific: If the harm reduction goal isn't concrete and specific, you, your loved one, and other harm reduction team members may be confused about exactly what you're all to do. A concrete and specific harm reduction goal describes when, where, and how to keep a harm reduction target clear. For example, a harm reduction goal might read, "Keep clutter out of the taped-off area in front of the stove" or "Keep clutter out of the taped area so that the front door can swing open and closed easily." The more concrete and specific the goal, the less likely that your loved one will postpone clearing the goal because she's confused about what she should or shouldn't do. In addition, the more concrete and specific the harm reduction goal, the less your loved one will worry whether she'll do it correctly.

Doable: By doable, we mean that the harm reduction goal is small enough that your loved one will likely be able to meet this goal. It'll be difficult enough for your loved one to keep even small areas clear of clutter. If you set harm reduction goals that are too difficult, you may decrease your loved one's confidence that harm reduction can help. For example, rather than asking your loved one to keep the kitchen floor clear of clutter, you might ask him to keep certain areas clear, such as in front of the stove or sink.

Prioritized: Most harm reduction goals fall into one of two categories: the *essential and immediate* and the *desired and longer term*. The essential and immediate goals focus on minimizing harm so that the person can live safely in her home. Desired and longer-term goals focus on improving the person's quality of life, her comfort level, or her relationships with friends and family members. Both types of goals are important, and both benefit your loved one's well-being. However, many times, your loved one will want to focus on the desired and longer-term goals rather than the essential and immediate goals, in part because she doesn't see that the latter goals are essential and immediate. For example, your loved one may prefer to clear the clutter from her bed so that she can sleep more comfortably, while ignoring the clutter on the stove top, which is a fire hazard. For this reason, we recommend that you prioritize harm reduction targets (see chapter 5) and always focus on those with the highest harm potential first.

Agree to a Plan for Monitoring

Even the best harm reduction plan will fail if no one monitors the conditions of the home. Monitoring includes both general home visits and methods for quickly monitoring specific harm reduction targets. You and your loved one will have to agree on the particular ways you'll monitor his progress with the harm reduction plan.

Ongoing monitoring through home visits is essential in order to identify and correct contract failures early, and reinforce ongoing progress in clearing and organizing tasks. In addition to promoting accountability, home visits boost motivation. Most people make it a point to tidy up when they expect visitors. Similarly, home visits often motivate people who hoard to put things in order and attend to the specific areas of the home that are harm reduction targets. We recommend a minimum of one home visit per month for adequate monitoring. Going longer than a month without checking progress can contribute to rapid worsening of ongoing problems. More frequent monitoring can help nip problems in the bud. Of course, some people who hoard require more frequent monitoring if the hoarding situation is extreme and you must quickly improve the safety of the living situation. The more frequent monitoring, the better, as long as the person who hoards doesn't experience the monitoring as overly frequent or obtrusive.

Monitoring also includes strategies for clearly specifying target areas. For example, you can mark off a rectangle in front of the stove or tape off a path through the kitchen with orange glow tape. In that way, you can quickly identify how well your loved one was able to keep a harm reduction target clear since your last visit. In addition, taped-off areas will remind your loved one not only to keep the area clear but also possibly to even work on other harm reduction targets. You can use tape in other ways to help you monitor progress toward a harm reduction goal. If a harm reduction goal is to keep the refrigerator clear of old food, you can date food stored in the refrigerator using tape and a marking pen. In this way, you and your loved one can quickly identify food that you agree to discard. You can tape off areas designated for other harm reduction activities. For example, you can mark with tape a rectangle on the floor in which your loved one agrees to keep the recycle bin at all times for easy access. You can tape off unsafe stairways or damaged areas of the home that your loved one agrees to stay out of until you can make the area safe.

However, you'll want to be able to monitor progress on other harm reduction targets that you can't mark off with tape, such as progress on recycling possessions rather than keeping them. Even a simple count of the number of boxes for recycling that you and your loved one fill during each home visit can help you see that you're making progress with the harm reduction plan.

Agree to Harm Reduction Strategies

In addition to harm reduction goals, your loved one's harm reduction plan will include all strategies you might use to reach those goals over time. For example, if a harm reduction goal is to decrease the flow of paper into your loved one's home, you might agree to a variety of harm reduction strategies to meet this goal. You might work with your loved one to ask companies to stop sending her paper bills or statements, and instead you can help her pay her bills online. If the power company often disconnects power to your loved one's home because she failed to pay her bill, you can work with her to pay essential bills (such as power, gas, telephone, and mortgage) automatically. Similarly, you can work with her to cancel some magazine subscriptions, make it easy for her to read the newspaper online, or get her off junk-mail or mail-order catalog lists.

STRATEGIES FOR REDUCING FINANCIAL RISK

You can include harm reduction strategies to decrease your loved one's financial risk by helping him find important documents—such as birth or death certificates, marriage or professional licenses, insurance policies, automobile and property titles, and wills and trusts—and helping him store these documents in a safe-deposit box at his bank. You can set up other systems to store important documents, such as tax returns, receipts for major purchases (such as furniture and electronics), and mutual-fund summaries. Working with your loved one to go through his mail regularly can also reduce the financial risks of falling behind on his rent, bills, or mortgage payments.

STRATEGIES FOR IMPROVING THE LIVING SITUATION

If you've identified improving the living situation itself as a harm reduction target, you might include in the harm reduction contract that you and your loved one agree to repair or replace whatever's broken. You might prioritize these items; for example, first, repair the air conditioner; second, repair the toilet; and third, repair the leaky roof. If you and your loved one have someone in mind to perform these repairs, list that person's name and contact information on the harm reduction plan.

STRATEGIES FOR ASSISTING WITH SAVING AND ORGANIZING

Other harm reduction strategies can focus on helping your loved one create systems for managing the hoarding problem. For example, you and your loved one can designate a small box or basket that she'll use to store items that she's to handle immediately. This "ASAP" box can hold bills to be paid or important papers to be filed within twenty-four hours. Similarly, you can set aside boxes for recycling, giving away, storing, and throwing away, which become harm reduction targets that you and your loved one agree to clear during home visits.

You and your loved one can create rules about what to save and for how long. For example, you and your loved one can set up other rules for keeping paper, such as six years for tax returns and year-end credit card statements; one year for monthly bank, credit card, or mutual-fund statements; and one month for credit-card receipts, withdrawal or deposit slips, and sales receipts for minor purchases. You can create rules for monitoring how many of an item to keep. For example, you can negotiate with your loved one to keep only as many plastic bags as will fit into one plastic bag, or as many empty water bottles or toilet-paper rolls as will fit in a single cardboard box. You can negotiate with your loved one about the number of clothes hangers to keep and agree that your loved one will keep only as many pants, coats, and shirts as will fit on that many hangers in his closet. These rules and strategies around keeping can remind your loved one to honor a limit you've negotiated together. In addition, these devices help you to quickly check how well your loved one is managing the hoarding problem. For example, if you set up a rule that all plastic bags are to be stored in a single plastic bag in the corner of the kitchen, you can quickly check whether your loved one honored that agreement.

You can set up rules about routines that your loved one will follow to help manage the hoarding problem. For example, creating a laundry day, a trash-takeout day, or a bill-paying day and highlighting these days on the calendar will help your loved one build the habit of staying on top of these daily, weekly, and monthly jobs. In addition, we know that daily cleaning, such as clearing the counters, sweeping the kitchen floor, and washing dishes helps keep surfaces uncluttered, because to clean a surface, you must clear it of clutter first. By scheduling these routine tasks, you'll help your loved one manage the clutter in her home.

You can find more about these strategies in other books about hoarding, as well as in numerous books on organizing and time management (see the appendix).

Formalizing the Harm Reduction Contract

The final step of the harm reduction plan is for you to formalize all the components into a harm reduction contract. A contract is a formal declaration by you, your loved one, and other team members that all will work to honor the terms of the harm reduction contract. Don't make the mistake of assuming that just because your loved one didn't openly *disagree* with the plan that he agreed to follow it. Saying nothing is not the same as agreeing. People tend to stick with a plan when they make a formal commitment to others to do it. For this reason, we recommend formalizing the components in a harm reduction contract that each harm reduction team member signs and dates. When introducing this to your loved one, you can say something like this: "It's important that all members of your team, including you, understand and agree to do their parts. I've put together a harm reduction contract that describes all the things we've discussed during the past meetings. I want to go over this with you and ask you to sign it. I'm asking you to sign first, because without your agreement, it doesn't really matter what other people agree to do. After you sign, I'll ask everyone else to sign. If you would prefer for the others to sign first, I'm certain that they would be happy to do that too."

Mary's Harm Reduction Contract

Harm Reduction Agreement

I, *Mary Smith* , and the other members of my harm reduction team understand that in order for me to continue to live safely and comfortably in my home, it is essential that I fully participate in the proposed harm reduction plan. To that end, I agree to the following:

- I will permit a designated harm reduction team member (referred to as "team member") to enter my home to assist me in keeping the designated harm reduction targets clear and honor all other harm reduction agreements. These home visits will occur weekly, or at a frequency designated in this harm reduction agreement. The current agreed-upon frequency of home visits is *twice* per month, beginning on *January 10, 2010.*

- I will permit the "team member" on each visit to photograph or videotape each room of my home and each area designated as a harm reduction goal for the purpose of monitoring my progress between home visits. The "team member" will not, without my permission, include me in the photos or videotape, and will use these images for the sole purpose of assisting me in managing my harm reduction plan.

- I will keep the following harm reduction targets clear and honor all other harm reduction agreements:

Safety Harm Reduction Targets

Clutter 24 inches away from top of stove.	Clutter 36 inches away from stair banister to second floor.
Clutter 12 inches away from furnace registers.	Clutter 36 inches away from stair banister to ground at back of house.
Will not use candles or open flames for lighting anywhere in house.	Will not use electric or gas space heaters anywhere in house.

Health and Comfort Harm Reduction Targets

Top of toilet and access to toilet clear so that toilet can be used.	Inside of shower and tub, and access to shower and tub, clear so that both can be used.
Food in refrigerator discarded after expiration date taped to food.	

■ I will accept the following accommodations and support:

Accommodations and Support

Delivery of meals-on-wheels and permit the driver to take food containers away.	All medications prescribed for my medical and emotional health.
Weekly visits by my sister, daughter (Martha), and the visiting nurse.	

■ I will accept help from the following professionals (referred to as "other professionals"):

Name of Professional	Purpose
Jane Good, visiting nurse	Wound care and routine medical evaluation and care
Dr. Albert Goff, psychiatrist	Medication management and psychotherapy
Roberta Austin, elder care worker	Harm reduction coach, decluttering, and monitor safety and comfort

■ I and the other team members will follow my harm reduction plan in good faith and in the spirit of ongoing negotiation to improve and maintain my health, safety, and comfort within my home.

Jane Good, RN	*Jane Good, RN* Signature	*1/10/10* Date
Ann Jones	*Ann Jones* Signature	*1/10/10* Date
John Hill, MD	*John Hill, MD* Signature	*1/10/10* Date

Regardless of the number of discussions you've had with your loved one, don't be surprised if he balks at signing the contract. If this happens, ask him why he's reluctant to sign a contract that he helped create. Perhaps he has some reservations about a particular team member or some part of the contract itself. Try to answer his questions as honestly and calmly as possible. Use L.E.A.P. to reassure him and enhance his confidence that you're there to help.

Remember, you haven't carved the details of the harm reduction contract in stone. Harm reduction contracts are evolving documents that the harm reduction team will revise over time. It's essential that everyone on the harm reduction team understand this. If you believe that a contract's a contract and that your loved one must follow the contract to the letter, you're in for a rough ride. We view a contract as an agreement between you and your loved one. Although the details of the contract are important, more important still is that you and your loved one come to an agreement that you formalize in a contract. The process of coming again and again to an agreement is a difficult but essential feature of the harm reduction approach.

DO'S AND DON'TS OF FORMING A CONTRACT

Do's	**Don'ts**
Do have all team members sign the contract. If a team member refuses to sign, she may not feel like a stakeholder. Review and clarify her goals for the harm reduction plan.	*Don't* argue about the contract. Instead, use L.E.A.P. to decrease defensiveness and negotiate an agreeable compromise (if possible).

Do explain that you and the team likely will revise the contract over time, depending on what comes up and how well the plan is working.	*Don't* threaten your loved one with an ultimatum in order to persuade her to sign the contract unless you intend to follow through with the threat.
Do praise your loved one for his willingness to enter into an agreement with you.	*Don't* use the contract or its process to intimidate your loved one. Try to keep the contract-forming process light and focused on helping your loved one live safely and comfortably in her home.
Do emphasize that the contract is there to help everyone keep on track, with the primary goal to help your loved one live safely and comfortably in his home.	*Don't* become rigid about the contract and demand that your loved one carry out every goal exactly as specified in the contract. Contracts change; can you?
Do include the frequency of home visits and other ways to monitor progress.	*Don't* move ahead with the harm reduction plan until everyone has signed the harm reduction contract. Nothing can take the harm reduction process off course faster than a team member who argues that he didn't agree with the terms of the contract.
Do remember to review the contract periodically and change it if needed.	*Don't* give up if you can't get all team members to sign the harm reduction contract. The contract-forming process is an essential part of the harm reduction approach. Use L.E.A.P. and take the time you need until everyone feels okay about the contents of the contract.

Do expect that no team member will be completely satisfied with the harm reduction contract. The contract represents many compromises and is not a perfect plan.	*Don't* expect a perfect plan. An imperfect harm reduction plan that all agree to honor is better than a perfect plan that few will honor.

If you or other members of the harm reduction team attach too tightly to a particular harm reduction contract, you won't be able to adjust to the many problems that will arise over the years. For example, the hoarding problem may begin as a private situation but soon become a public one. Once public, you can expect an authority to appear and insist that he join the harm reduction team. This new team member will likely have new goals and new ideas that he'll want you to incorporate into your loved one's harm reduction plan. A new plan means negotiating a new harm reduction contract. Alternatively, the harm reduction contract might change because one or more harm reduction targets have changed. For example, a harm reduction contract might prohibit your loved one from using space heaters to heat her home. However, after someone repairs the furnace, your loved one is less likely to want to use space heaters for heat. Instead, keeping the furnace registers clear of clutter is a new harm reduction goal. It's essential that you be able to change the harm reduction contract to adjust for increases or decreases in your loved one's harm potential, as well as for changes in the harm reduction team. Before or after you and your loved one sign the harm reduction contract, underscore the importance that all team members view the contract in the same way—as an agreement that's likely to change over time. For example, state the following:

This is a working document. We expect it to change as we move ahead with the harm reduction plan. Our willingness to work together to honor the terms of the contract is important. However, as important is our willingness to work together to negotiate a new contract. We expect new contracts and new agreements. The goal is always to have a harm reduction contract in play and to try to follow the terms of that contract. However, because we cannot know ahead of time the changes we may need to make to your harm reduction plan, we cannot expect the same contract to get the job done. I hope we can all agree to work together to negotiate new contracts as needed.

111

At the last minute, your loved one might balk. This is understandable because the contract represents her commitment to make significant changes. She might refuse to sign the contract when, only a day earlier, she said she would sign. This is a crucial test of your patience. L.E.A.P. back into the discussion (see chapter 4) and clarify her reasons for refusing to sign now. Listen to her concerns. Empathize with her fears. If your loved one has doubts about whether she can follow the terms of the contract, remind her that the contract can change and that you don't know whether this is the best contract for her. Time will tell, because neither of you can predict what changes you'll need to make in order to help her manage the hoarding problem. If your loved one asserts that she feels boxed in by the contract, remind her that the contract includes her input too and that the contract actually gives her more, not less, control of how she manages the hoarding problem.

In this chapter, you learned the general features of a harm reduction plan, which include realistic harm reduction goals as well as a variety of harm reduction strategies you and other team members will use to manage the hoarding problem. In addition, you learned how to go about putting together an effective harm reduction team that's committed to helping your loved one over the long term. Finally, you learned how to create a harm reduction contract that will guide you and other team members through the ups and downs of managing your loved one's hoarding problem. The following chapter describes how to work effectively with your loved one to clear harm reduction targets and honor other features of the harm reduction contract.

CHAPTER 7

Keeping the Harm Reduction Targets Clear

Recluttered harm reduction targets is the most common form of contract failure. In this chapter, we present seven steps to follow when working with your loved one to clear harm reduction targets. In addition, we introduce L.E.A.R.N. as a way to discuss these kinds of contract failures with your loved one, as well as other strategies to help your loved one clear harm reduction targets.

Step Carefully: Seven Steps to Successful Home Visits

When it comes to harm reduction, you and your loved one are in it for the long haul. In your loved one's harm reduction contract, you've agreed upon the inclusion of home visits and how often they happen. How you handle these home visits will determine whether you and your loved one sink or swim. Because these home visits will continue (at some agreed-upon frequency) as long as your loved one struggles with her hoarding problem, it's essential to have a structure to guide you. In addition, since other team members will take turns assisting your loved one with keeping the harm reduction targets clear, it helps when everyone conducts home visits in the same way. To make every home visit as successful as possible, we recommend that you and other harm reduction team members follow these seven steps.

Step 1: Review the Harm Reduction Contract

Prior to visiting your loved one's home, it's worth taking a few minutes to review the harm reduction contract. During a home visit, you'll likely spend the most time reviewing your loved one's progress in keeping the harm reduction targets clear that are specified in his contract. However, you may want to follow up on other important pieces of your loved one's harm reduction contract. For example, you might want to check your loved one's progress on removing his name from junk-mail lists, or shifting to paying his bills online and requesting paperless (electronic) statements.

Use a three-ring binder to store your Home Visit Worksheets (introduced later in this chapter). This is a record of your and your loved one's progress. It's like the medical chart that the nurses and physicians keep with a patient in the hospital. Any medical staff member who wants to check on the patient's status can read the chart and know what care the patient has received and by whom. It saves time, keeps the lines of communication clear, and often avoids the "he said, she said" effect when you want to know where other team members left things during the last visit. We organize the binder into sections: contracts (for current and past revisions of the harm reduction contract), home visits (for past Home Visit Worksheets), and communication (for notes to other team members).

Step 2: Monitor Each Harm Reduction Target

Once in the home, be warm and polite, but don't chitchat, because you'll want to save this until you and your loved one have completed the harm reduction work. As you walk through the home, examine progress on each harm reduction target and look for potential new targets to include in your loved one's harm reduction plan. Don't start work on clearing any harm reduction target yet. Examine them all before deciding which one you'll take up first. Remember, you've rated the harm reduction targets (see chapter 5) according to risk and discomfort, and you want to start with the targets with the highest risk and discomfort numbers first. We like to evaluate the status of each target on a scale from 1 to 5 (where each number equals ten minutes of clearing time). That means that if you rate a target at 4, you've estimated that it'll take you and your loved one about forty minutes to clear the area to the standard specified in the harm reduction contract. Note these estimates on the Home Visit Worksheet. Most home visits run about an hour, because an hour is the most your loved one can likely tolerate, particularly at first. In addition, you want to have ten minutes or so to socialize with your loved one at the end of the home visit.

Step 3: Praise All Approximations to the Desired Goal

The philosophy of harm reduction is that any positive change counts. Managing a serious hoarding problem over time is not a sprint but a marathon, and like any difficult long-term endeavor, your loved one won't always succeed completely. Most likely, as you review the harm reduction targets, you'll see small changes or partial attempts to keep the harm reduction targets clear. However, particularly if you're making regular home visits to monitor progress on the harm reduction plan, it's not likely that the area looks the way it did when you first visited to assess your loved one's harm potential. For that reason, we encourage you to praise all efforts your loved one makes to keep the target areas clear. Even if the area looks about the same as it did during the last visit, praise your loved one for not adding more clutter to the area: "It's great that you didn't place more stuff near the stove, as we agreed. Let's try to build on that and get some more stuff out of this area. What do you think?"

We recommend paying attention to a few things when you praise your loved one's efforts. First, don't qualify your praise (for example, "I'm so glad you cleared this area as we agreed. Why can't you do that more often?"), inadvertently criticizing your loved one. Second, praise a specific behavior (for example, "I like how you kept the newspapers off the stairs this week") rather than give global praise (such as, "You're doing a great job").

Step 4: Clear Harm Reduction Target

Once you and your loved one have moved to clearing or reclearing a harm reduction target, you'll want to keep your role as simple as possible. We suggest focusing on two things during every visit. First, help your loved one stay focused on clearing the harm reduction targets or on any other task that's part of a routine home visit. Often, people who hoard are easily distracted, especially when they're working with you to clear a target area. Your loved one may be anxious, tired, or both. Her motivation may be lower than the last visit, or she may seem to have more trouble deciding what to keep, how to keep it, and whether it makes sense to discard something. During these moments, your job is to gently and politely remind your loved one to refocus on the present task: "You were making good progress in clearing this area. Let's get back to what we were doing. Would that be okay?"

Second, as you work on a particular target area, you'll encounter any number of problems that you and your loved one will need to solve, including disagreements or misunderstandings that can affect your working relationship. Later in this chapter, we'll teach you L.E.A.R.N., which is a model to help you think through these problems and to work effectively with your loved one to stay on the task of clearing or reclearing the target areas.

Step 5: Revise and Agree on New or Modified Harm Reduction Targets

Because you and your loved one are in this for the long term, it's essential that you both keep an open mind and be willing to brainstorm new ways to keep harm reduction targets clear. At times, this is as simple as agreeing to adjust a target area, such as agreeing to keep the area next to the staircase banister clear of clutter rather than the entire staircase. Alternatively, you might want to consider new ways of managing the clutter that comes into the home or to call on other people to serve as harm reduction team members.

Step 6: End on the Positive

We believe that having a positive and caring relationship with you is a primary motivator for your loved one to work with you on the hoarding problem. For that reason, we recommend ending every home visit with some social time with your loved one. You don't need to spend a great deal of time with your loved one, just ten minutes or so at the end of the home visit to chat and catch up. In fact, you may want to think about using the social time to reward your loved one for working hard on the hoarding problem, spending less social time when your loved one has worked less hard. You can say, "Wow. We only have five minutes to chat today because we spent so much time reclearing the area in front of the stove. Maybe on the next visit we won't have to spend so much time reclearing that area, and we'll have more time to visit. I hope so."

During the social time, try to socialize in an area of the home that you and your loved one have cleared or recleared, and try to do an activity in the cleared area. For example, if you and your loved one have cleared the area near the stove, use the stove to make tea or bake cookies. Don't talk about the hoarding problem during this social time. Spend the time catching up on family news (ask about the grandchildren or fun things your loved one has done since your last visit). If you remember something about the hoarding problem that you want to discuss with your loved one before you leave, reserve that for the checkout period, when you schedule the next home visit.

Step 7: Set a Date for the Next Home Visit

At the end of the social time, take a few minutes to agree on the date of the next home visit and write that down for your loved one. If you know which team member will visit next, let your loved one know and discuss with him what he'll do to work on the hoarding problem before the next visit. Write these tasks down and post them in a visible and easily accessible place.

If your loved one is worried about the next visit or about the next team member, spend some time listening to her concerns and reassuring her. If she hasn't met a team member, arrange a telephone conversation or even a brief social visit well in advance of the harm reduction home visit. In general, try to avoid having a home visit be the first time your loved one meets a new team member. Meeting someone new on neutral ground will likely be far more comfortable for a person who hoards. Last, remember to praise your loved one again for her efforts and for her commitment to working with you on the harm reduction problem.

Home Visit Worksheet

Date of visit: _____ **Name of team member:** _____

Directions: As you walk through the home, take note of how well your loved one has done to keep each harm reduction target clear. In addition, look for potential new targets to include in your loved one's harm reduction contract. Don't start work on clearing any harm reduction target until you have examined all the targets. Rate each harm reduction target according to risk on a 1 to 10 scale (where 10 is "extreme risk"). Note these estimates on the Home Visit Worksheet in the Priority column. Estimate the time needed to clear each target on a scale from 1 to 5 (where each number equals ten minutes of clearing time). That means that if you rate a target at 4, you've estimated that it will take you and your loved one about forty minutes to clear the area to the standard specified in the harm reduction contract. Note these estimates on the Home Visit Worksheet in the Time Estimate column. Always begin with the highest priority target.

Harm Reduction Targets	Priority (1 to 10)	Time Estimate (1 to 5)

Notes and Comments:

_____

_____

_____

_____

_____

_____

_____

_____

_____

_____

Date of next home visit: _____

Why Do You Have This *Here*?

A principle difference between treatment and harm reduction is how someone who's working with a person who hoards begins the work of clearing a cluttered area. If you're a therapist and focused on treating the hoarding problem, you might point to a possession and ask, "Why do you have this?" Someone focused on harm reduction, on the other hand, might point to a possession and ask, "Why do you have this *here?*"

Now, you might think that there's little difference between these two opening gambits, but there's a world of difference, because each phrase moves the conversation along different lines. When you ask your loved one, "Why do you have this?" the goal of this question is to open a discussion about the value of keeping or discarding an item. In so doing, you invite the person who hoards to explain the reasons why he's keeping the item. If the person has sought help for his hoarding problem, this conversation can move to other conversations through which the therapist helps the person quickly and effectively make decisions about keeping or discarding, and then go on to sorting, categorizing, and employing other strategies your loved one can use to declutter and manage his hoarding problem. However, if you ask that question of someone who has *not* sought help because he doesn't see that he has a significant hoarding problem, the conversation can quickly dissolve into debating the merits of keeping the item or not. Soon, the person becomes guarded and defensive, and the process of clearing the area stalls.

Although discarding items is certainly a goal of harm reduction, it's not the primary goal. Instead, harm reduction strives for managing possessions to minimize harm. When you ask your loved one, "Why do you have this *here*?" you invite her to discuss the merits of keeping the possession in that spot, rather than some other place that might present less risk to her. In so doing, you set the stage for a different kind of conversation during the clearing visit, one focused on safety and comfort rather than overfocused on decluttering the living environment. In addition, you move the discussion to brainstorming for other solutions, which is the hallmark of effective problem solving.

L.E.A.R.N.: Listen, Empathize, Affirm, Redirect, and Negotiate

In this section, we present a five-step model to help you work with your loved one in a caring and collaborative way to clear the harm reduction targets during your home visits. You'll notice that the first three steps of L.E.A.R.N. (listen, empathize, and affirm) and L.E.A.P. (listen, empathize, and agree) are similar. Rather than describe these steps in detail again, we focus instead on how to apply them to keeping harm reduction targets clear. If you want to refresh your memory about L.E.A.P., feel free to go back and reread chapter 4.

As you apply L.E.A.R.N.—listen, empathize, affirm, redirect, and negotiate—to helping your loved one clear harm reduction targets, it may help you to think about each step of L.E.A.R.N. as a rung on a ladder. As you work to clear a target area, you'll find yourself moving up and down this ladder, from the bottom rung (listen) to the top rung (negotiate). Many times, you may move up and down between the first and third rungs (listen and affirm) or between the fourth and fifth (redirect and negotiate). Going up and down these rungs can be exhausting. However, in so doing, you keep your relationship with your loved one foremost in your mind. Without a good working relationship, you won't be able to do the work that keeps him safe and comfortable.

Listen

Listening actively involves paraphrasing, clarifying, and giving feedback. Let's quickly see how each of these features of listening applies to working with your loved one to clear a harm reduction target.

Paraphrasing: Remember, to paraphrase, you open with a declaration of what you heard but let your loved one know that it's possible that you heard wrong. Let's look at how Ted paraphrased when talking to his mother about the location of the tape recorder:

Ted: "Mom, why do you keep the tape recorder and tapes here?"

Laura: "Well, I keep my radio here so that I can listen to my favorite programs when I cook. Sometimes I want to tape a program and need to have the tape recorder and tapes nearby so I can do that. I know it's not the best place for it, but I couldn't find anyplace else that would work."

Ted: "You know this isn't a good place for it. Are you open to finding someplace else to put it?"

Laura: "Yes. I know it's not safe to keep so many tapes next to the stove top, but where else could I put them?"

Ted: "You're looking for a safer place to put them?"

Laura: "Yes, safer would be good, but I don't want to throw them out. Don't tell me to do that."

Ted: "I want to get this straight: you're open to finding a safer place for the tapes as long as I don't tell you to throw any of them out. Is that right?"

Laura: "Well, I don't want you to tell me to throw all of them out, but there may be one or two that are old and damaged."

As you can see, Ted opened the door a bit for he and his mother to brainstorm all options for clearing the area, including perhaps throwing away a few old and damaged tapes. Through paraphrasing, Ted communicated to his mother that he was listening. This helped Laura feel more at ease and thereby more open to working with her son to do what it would take to keep her safe.

Clarifying: Clarifying helps keep the conversation with your loved one on track by helping you to catch a listening error early. Remember though, you're not interrogating your loved one or pressuring him to see things the way you do. You want to communicate that you're interested in understanding and helping your loved one, not in winning a debate. Let's see how Ted clarifies to keep the conversation with his mother on track:

Laura: "Well, I don't want you to tell me to throw all of them out, but there may be one or two that are old and damaged."

Ted: "So, you're ready to throw the damaged tapes out?"

Laura: "No. We might talk about throwing the damaged tapes out. I'm not agreeing to throw any tapes out."

Ted: "I'm sorry. I misunderstood you. Are you open to throwing out some damaged tapes?"

Laura: "I'm open to talking to you about it."

Ted: "So, talking about throwing away a tape is the first step. What else would you need in order to feel comfortable about throwing away a tape?"

Laura: "I guess I would want us to agree about when a tape is damaged so much that it can't be repaired."

Ted: "So, we're really talking about throwing away tapes that are damaged beyond repair. Is that right?"

Laura: "Yes, I think I could throw a badly damaged tape away."

Giving feedback: Feedback is your time to, calmly and without judgment, share your own thoughts, feelings, opinions, and desires with your loved one about what she said. Ted has learned how to give his mother feedback in a caring and supportive way:

Laura: "I'm open to talking to you about throwing some damaged tapes away. That's all."

Ted: "I feel as if you just closed the door when you said, 'That's all.' I know you want me to hear that you make the final call on what we keep and what we discard, but it upsets me when you close the door like that."

Laura: "You're right. I'm sorry, but sometime I worry that you're going to start pushing me to throw things out the way you used to, that's all. I'm sorry."

Active Listening Practice

In this exercise, you'll, again, practice active listening, the first step in L.E.A.R.N. You've already learned how to listen actively when trying to help your loved one accept help (chapter 4), but in this exercise, you'll use active listening when helping your loved one clear a target area. Practice with another family member, friend, or other team member. One of you will play the role of the team member, and the other will play the role of your loved one. The conversation will focus on clearing a target area. Remember to include the three features of active listening: paraphrasing, clarifying, and giving feedback. Ask the person who plays the role of the family member to take it easy on you at first. Later, after you've had more practice at listening actively, the person playing your family member can turn up the heat a bit by becoming defensive or trying to argue with you. After each role-play, give each other feedback and try again until you feel confident that you can listen actively to help your loved one clear harm reduction targets.

Empathize

Showing empathy means trying to understand how someone thinks and feels. In conversations focused on keeping the harm reduction targets clear, showing empathy means trying to understand why your loved one wasn't able to keep the area clear and how he feels about his inability to do this. Showing empathy can lead to new information about your loved one's hoarding problem that may result in new ways to help. More important, however, showing empathy demonstrates that you care and understand how hard it is to work on the problem. Watch Ted as he shows empathy for his mother's failed attempt to keep a harm reduction target clear:

Laura: "I'm sorry. Things just piled up on the stairs. I meant to move them upstairs, but I just didn't have time."

Ted: "You meant to keep the stairs clear, but you didn't have time. It looks as if you're feeling anxious right now. Are you?"

Laura: "Well, yes, a little. I know I agreed to keep the stairs clear, and I like to keep my promises."

Ted: "Yes. That's one of the wonderful things about you, Mom: you always try to do what you said you were going to do. It must be frustrating not to be able to do that all the time when it comes to keeping the clutter down."

Laura: "Yes, it really is. I knew this was going to be hard, but I thought I could at least keep the stairs clear of stuff. I'm sorry. I'll try more this week."

Ted: "That would be great, Mom. Is there something I can do to help with that?"

Affirm

When working with your loved one to clear a harm reduction target, you won't always agree, nor should you. When you do agree with your loved one, say so: "Yes, this is really hard to do" or "Yes, this is taking us more time than I thought it would." However, even when you can't agree, you can affirm what your loved one says to you. Affirming, in the way we think of it, means you simply let your loved one know that you heard what she said: "Yes, that magazine article is important to you." You can affirm a great many things. You can affirm that she loves a possession and can't let go of it: "It's hard for you to let go of that." You can affirm that she doesn't want to work any longer on clearing the area: "You can't work on this anymore." You can even affirm that she believes she doesn't have a problem: "You're happy with the way things are." Affirming what your loved one says keeps you both focused on clearing rather than talking about clearing. Affirming avoids debating fine points. Affirming sidesteps conversations about where your loved one purchased an item or how long ago she last saw it. Although these conversations strengthen your relationship with your loved one, too many of them can slow down the clearing task. Affirming enables you to graciously and politely redirect your loved one back to clearing the harm reduction targets.

Redirect

As you and your loved one work to clear a target area, your loved one may want to chat or make a cup of tea for you instead of clearing. Every few moments, he may want to take a break or may get up and roam around the house looking for something. When this happens, gently redirect your loved one back to clearing the area. Politely and gently say, "Now it's time to get back to clearing this target area. Are you ready?" If you're working on a particular area, you can point and say, "You're doing a great job. How about if we work a few more minutes on this before we take a break?" Often, your loved one will want to talk about a possession rather than deal with it. It's wiser to save these discussions for the social time at the end of the home visit: "Yes, Mom, I bet you have a great story about these ticket stubs. Why don't you tell me the story later, after we've finished clearing? I promise to remind you, because I want to hear about it." Most times, particularly when your loved one has simply drifted away from the task, this will be enough.

At other times, the clearing process will stall because your loved one's motivation has decreased, or she's become argumentative or defensive. At these times, you want to move back to the first three steps of L.E.A.R.N. (listen, empathize, and affirm) before redirecting your loved one back to clearing the target area. Remember, the primary goal of L.E.A.R.N. is to, in a caring and collaborative way, work through the many obstacles that arise when helping your loved one clear and reclear harm reduction targets. Often, listening, empathizing, and affirming will lower your loved one's defensiveness enough for her to accept redirection back to the clearing task. After you listen, empathize, and affirm, gently and politely say, "I'm glad we talked that through. Are we ready to get back to clearing this area together?"

Negotiate

You won't always need to negotiate with your loved one while clearing a target area, particularly if you've negotiated and agreed upon a general plan. For example, you may have negotiated and agreed that you'll move the newspapers in the target area to a box that you'll then place outside to be recycled. However, you'll often need to negotiate a myriad of other things when helping your loved one clear the target area. For example, you may need to negotiate whether to stop or continue clearing a bit longer, or negotiate what to discard or keep and how to store it. You may need to negotiate where to move something and how, or negotiate a safer place or a safer way to store something. Negotiating is an essential part of L.E.A.R.N., but the early steps set the stage for these negotiations. Now, look at how Ted puts the five steps of L.E.A.R.N. together and how he walks up and down this ladder to keep the door open and stay on the task of helping his mother clear a target area.

Laura: "I don't want to do this anymore. I'm tired."

Ted: "This clearing has really taken it out of you. What is it about the clearing that's hard for you?" [Ted paraphrases and then asks his mother to clarify what she means.]

Laura: "Well, it's exhausting, and you want me to do this more than I want to do this."

Ted: "I hear you saying that you feel that I'm pushing you. Is that right?"

Laura: "Yes. I think this area looks fine. I don't see the point of doing more."

Ted: "I know this must be frustrating for you sometimes. We don't always see things the same way when it comes to your possessions, but I thought we agreed that we would work together to keep you safe. Keeping you safe in your home is the most important thing to me. That's what I thought we were doing. Did I miss something?" [Ted empathizes with his mother and then gives her feedback.]

Laura: "Yes, we agreed to focus on keeping me safe. I remember, but sometimes I think you're pushing me too hard."

Ted: "Yes. You feel pushed by me. Can you tell me what I'm doing that feels as if I'm pushing you? If I can change it, I will." [Ted affirms and then redirects his mother to solving the problem of her feeling pushed.]

Laura: "Well, maybe if you slowed down. Why do we have to do this so quickly? I have to make so many decisions that it's just overwhelming sometimes."

Ted: "One option would be to slow down. I could do that. Do you think we'll be able to clear this area in time if I slow down? I have to leave in forty minutes, and I want to leave time to chat with you." [Ted begins to negotiate. He affirms that he could slow down but also points out that it will slow them down in meeting their goal. In addition, he points out another consequence of slowing down, which is having less time for socializing at the end of the home visit.]

Laura: "I know it'll slow us down. That's part of my frustration. Everything seems to take so long."

Ted: "Yes, it does take time, and I understand how frustrating that is for you. It frustrates me a little too sometimes. Do you have any other ideas about how you can not feel pushed by me?" [Ted empathizes with his mother, affirms, and redirects her back to more brainstorming and negotiating.]

Laura: "I don't know. Maybe if we just took a two-minute break. That's all I need, just two minutes to catch my breath."

Ted: "That's a great idea. Why don't you take a two-minute breather, and I'll continue to work on this area, if that's all right with you. Is it okay?"

Laura: "Yes. I'll sit here and watch."

In the previous example, Ted used L.E.A.R.N. to help his mother stay on track with the clearing task. Now, watch Ted use L.E.A.R.N. to clear an item out of the target area. Ted begins the process by pointing to a small stack of newspapers in the target area in front of the stove.

Ted: "Mom, why do you have these here?"

Laura: "I know, I know. They're not supposed to be there, but I was reading the newspaper at the kitchen table, and I guess I just let the papers drop there. I'm sorry."

Ted: "You were enjoying the newspaper while you were having breakfast. That's great! In particular, it's great that you're able to sit at the breakfast table again to read your paper. I know it's tough to stay on top of the clutter the way you want, but keeping newspapers in this area is really risky." [Ted listens, empathizes, and affirms. He also redirects his mother to her agreement to keep this area clear of newspapers.]

Laura: "I know. It won't happen again, I promise."

Ted: "Mom, I really appreciate that you're willing to honor your agreement with me. I really do, but maybe we should look at this situation and see if we can come up with a plan to help you out with the newspapers. Would that be okay?" [Ted redirects his mother to finding a solution to the newspaper problem and begins to negotiate a strategy that might help.]

Laura: "Okay, but I promised I wouldn't do it again."

Ted: "I know, Mom, and I appreciate your wanting to work on this, but if we can find a way to make that easier, wouldn't that be better for you? So, it sounds as if you don't intend to keep these newspapers here. They sometimes drift here when you're reading at breakfast time. Is that right?" [Again, Ted affirms and redirects his mother back to problem solving.]

Laura: "Yes. I kind of get distracted."

Ted: "How about this idea? How about if we placed a recycling container under the breakfast table so that you can drop the newspapers there? The box doesn't have to be big, just a little one that I can help you take outside during my visits. How would that work?"

Laura: "That might work. Yes, I like that idea."

Practice L.E.A.R.N.

In this exercise, you'll put it all together and apply L.E.A.R.N. to helping your loved one clear a harm reduction target. You may want to practice with another family member, friend, or other team member before you try it with your loved one. One of you will play the role of the team member, and the other will play the role of your loved one. The conversation will focus on clearing a target area. Remember to begin the conversation with, "Why do you have this *here*?" and use L.E.A.R.N. to keep the conversation on track. The person who plays your loved one can take it easy on you at first, but later, after you've had more practice using L.E.A.R.N., the person playing your loved one can make it a little more difficult for you by becoming defensive or arguing with you. After each role-play, give each other feedback and try again until you feel confident that you can L.E.A.R.N. to help your loved one clear harm reduction targets.

Skills for the Long Term

As with any problem, it takes certain skills to manage a hoarding problem. For example, your loved one must be able to organize his possessions and make many decisions about them, such as what to keep and what to discard. If he keeps something, he must decide how to store it and where, and through it all, he must manage his time effectively so that he doesn't spend too much time on less important tasks. People who hoard often have problems in these areas.

Assist with Sorting and Organizing

You may look around your loved one's home and think she's the most disorganized person you've ever met. However, that's not necessarily the case. People with hoarding problems actually try to organize their possessions, but the strategies they use are ineffective for the task. For example, people who hoard often try to organize their possessions by trying to keep everything in sight. This means, rather than place papers or receipts in a drawer or filing cabinet, they organize their possessions on every horizontal surface they can find to keep it in view, so that they won't forget or misplace it. In addition, people who hoard can't categorize their possessions effectively, because they see many, if not most, of their possessions as unique or special. Imagine trying to file a hundred postcards if you believed that every postcard was unique. You would need a hundred file folders, right? We tell you this only to help you see that the problem is not that your loved one is unable to organize her possessions but rather that she's unable to organize her possessions effectively.

In addition, most people who hoard can't organize their possessions effectively because they don't have space to do it since they've covered the floors, desks, tabletops, and most horizontal surfaces with paper and other possessions. Therefore, one of the first steps toward helping your loved one organize his possessions is to designate an "organization station" in the home. The harm reduction team then works to keep this space clear for sorting and organizing possessions only. Next, you and your loved one will want to gather a few things to make the sorting and organizing easier. Although every situation is different, here are a few things that harm reduction team members will want to have on hand and put in place.

Checklist: Preparing to Clear Target Areas

Supplies:

- ☐ Boxes or storage containers. Clear are best, because you and your loved one will be able to see the contents when they're stacked or stored. If you don't use clear storage containers or boxes, you'll need labels and pens.

- ☐ Boxes marked "Recycle," "Sell," and "Donate."

- ☐ Garbage bags for trash. Large leaf bags and smaller kitchen bags are great.

- ☐ Recycle bins for recycling newspaper, bottles, and cans.

- ☐ File folders, hanging files, and filing cabinets (if you'll be sorting and filing).

Things to Do:

- ☐ Rent a Dumpster if you expect to clear out a lot of paper or material. This would likely happen during the early home visits, if needed. Check the Yellow Pages or online for a list of trash-hauling companies that will deliver and remove a Dumpster from your loved one's home.

- ☐ Clear a work or staging area. You'll use this for sorting and organizing things that you remove from the harm reduction targets. If you can't find uncluttered space near the target areas, try using the porch, backyard, or an outside hallway. This is only a temporary location, and you must clear the staging area by the end of the home visit.

☐ Call your loved one and confirm the date and time of the home visit.

☐ If other team members are helping you, call them and confirm that they can make the home visit, and alert them to the date and time.

Assist with Creative Problem Solving

Difficulty solving the day-to-day problems that arise when trying to manage a hoarding problem can make it difficult for your loved one to honor his harm reduction contract, even when he's very motivated to do this. To solve problems effectively, your loved one must be able to think flexibly. By that we mean that your loved one must have the ability to consider all possible solutions to a particular problem. If your loved one can't do this, then he may give up when working to clear harm reduction targets.

When your loved one fails to honor her contract, such as neglecting to keep a harm reduction target clear, be ready to help find a creative solution to the problem. Where could she move the pile? How could she organize new possessions coming into the home so that the specified target area doesn't get recluttered? What kind of system would help her stay on top of the clutter?

Assist with Decision Making

People who hoard often have trouble making decisions, small ones and big ones. They think and rethink what to keep and what to remove from the home. They decide and then change their minds about where to keep something or how to categorize it. For example, "Do I file it under 'Plumbing' or 'Home Repairs'?" As a member of the harm reduction team, your job is to help your loved one make certain decisions and, failing that, to obtain his permission to make those decisions yourself.

Helping your loved one decide what to clear: Perhaps the biggest decision your loved one faces when she thinks about working on the hoarding problem is what area of her home to clear. Deciding where to start isn't as easy as it might seem, particularly when you remember what her home looks like. However, the harm reduction plan sidesteps this problem, because you and your loved one have decided which areas (the harm reduction targets) are to be cleared well ahead of the first clearing visit. In addition, as you've learned, at the beginning of each home visit, you've prioritized the target areas and estimated the amount of time needed to clear the area. This will help you and your loved one stay on track and use the clearing time effectively.

Helping your loved one decide to stay on track: Even if your loved one has agreed to keep the target areas clear, he'll have trouble staying on track. You may notice that as you and he begin working on one area, he drifts over to another target area to work, or over to another pile of papers where he sifts and churns the contents of the pile. In addition, he may become overwhelmed and sit down after only a few minutes. Clearing is a difficult task, and your loved one may feel anxious, disoriented, or even frustrated. Your job is to keep the ball rolling, even if your loved one simply sits and observes. However, always follow the rule of touching only with permission.

Helping your loved one decide what to do with a possession: Although your goal is modest—to clear high-risk target areas and keep them clear—this can be tedious at times because of the difficulty your loved one may have with making decisions. Many times, the decision will be about where to move something rather than whether to discard it. However, storing, discarding, or moving an item out of the home is a goal too, and we encourage you to try to move items out of the home when your loved one is open to it. To that end, we use a series of decision-making questions. Stepping through these questions with your loved one takes time and patience. However, over time and after several home visits, you may notice that your loved one is able to make decisions more quickly and with less assistance from you.

DECISION-MAKING QUESTIONS

For Clearing and Moving	For Clearing, Storing, or Discarding
Why do you have this here?	Why do you have this?
Is there another place where we might put this?	Do you need this?
If you can't do without it, can we pick another place for it?	Can you do without it?

For Clearing and Moving	For Clearing, Storing, or Discarding
Is it safe for you to keep this here?	How many of these do you already have, and is that enough?
Does keeping this make you more uncomfortable in your home?	Do you have enough space for this?
Is it safe for you to keep this or to keep so many of these?	Do you have enough time to actually use, read, or go over it?
	When was the last time you thought about this?
	Would you buy it again if you didn't already own it?
	Could you get it again if you found that you really needed it?
	Do you have enough space for this?
	Will you use this item in the next week, month, or year?
	Have you used this in the past year?

Helping your loved one decide to let go of a possession: To keep the target areas clear over the long term, your loved one must let go of some things, and your job is to help him do this. It can help for you and your loved one to develop some simple rules about letting go of possessions. These rules can sidestep the circular and time-consuming process of trying to decide what to keep and what to discard for each possession in the target area. Ideally, you and your loved one will have decided on these rules early and included them in the harm reduction contract. If not, you can develop these rules during the first few home visits.

You and your loved one can create rules for anything. For example, you and your loved one might agree that when newspapers are more than a week old, you recycle them whether or not your loved one has read them. You can create rules about when to discard food stored in the refrigerator. For example, your loved one may agree to discard any food item stored past the expiration date that you write on the package.

Helping your loved one decide to work without help from others: Ideally, your loved one will work to keep the target areas clear between visits. We say "ideally" because we don't expect this from most people who accept a harm reduction approach since they're often the least motivated and most impaired. Certainly, we wouldn't expect much effort on your loved one's part during the early months of the harm reduction contract. Nonetheless, we recommend that you ask that of your loved one, and having clearly defined harm reduction targets will help. For the harm reduction target, you'll negotiate with your loved one and agree on how much time each month she'll spend clearing the areas. For some people, you may want to clearly identify the day and time each month. To help your loved one follow through with her commitment to clear the target areas on her own, you might call to check on her progress between your home visits.

In this chapter, you learned the seven steps to successful home visits, which will help you make every visit effective and positive. In addition, you were introduced to L.E.A.R.N., a communication strategy that you'll use repeatedly when working with your loved one to clear and reclear target areas. Finally, you learned several skills, such as how to help your loved one quickly and efficiently make decisions about his many possessions. The following chapter describes how to manage the many twists, turns, and bumps that will arise over time as you work to help your loved one manage the hoarding problem.

CHAPTER 8

Managing the Bumps
in the Road

If you're reading this book, you're no doubt concerned about your loved one and invested in finding ways to help her succeed in changing. However, the path to success is seldom straight and unwavering. Most people take a few steps forward with their harm reduction contracts and then a few steps back.

In this chapter, we describe six common reasons for contract failures and offer tips for working through them. We also discuss bumps in the road outside of the scope of the harm reduction contract, such as deciding whether to make a private hoarding situation public. Finally, we discuss the pros and cons associated with taking private hoarding situations public.

Six Common Reasons for Contract Failures

Over the years, we've observed that harm reduction contracts typically fail for one of six reasons.

Reason 1: The Contract Wasn't Set Collaboratively

A harm reduction contract will likely fail when it doesn't include the most important goals of one or more members of the harm reduction team. Early harm reduction contract negotiations are critical. They set the tone for future discussions with your loved one when he or another member of his harm reduction team fails to honor the contract. Remember, however, that no contract is perfect and that not everyone will be completely satisfied. Instead, you're working toward a contract that has enough of what each stakeholder wants so that each person is willing to move ahead.

TIPS FOR GETTING BACK ON TRACK

- Don't move ahead with the harm reduction plan until you have a contract that all members of the harm reduction team have agreed to. If not, break goals down into smaller subgoals that everyone can agree to.

- Expect and accept that you'll have goals for the person who hoards that she and some team members don't share. Working with a trusted clinician can help the group mediate its goals and work through differences.

Reason 2: The Contract Was Unrealistic

An unrealistic harm reduction contract likely has perfectionistic goals that make it difficult for your loved one to succeed. For example, Brad, a fifty-five-year-old software engineer, placed his cherished engineering journals on the kitchen countertop so that he would see them throughout the day. The journals loomed dangerously close to the stove top and posed a fire hazard when he and his family cooked their meals. Brad considered setting the contract goal: "No journals in the kitchen." However, Brad's father, who was also on the team, saw straightaway that this would be an unrealistic goal. Instead, the team agreed that a better goal would be: "No more than two journals on the counter, and both must be at least six inches away from the stove top."

Your loved one isn't the only one who'll fall into the trap of setting unrealistic harm reduction goals. You and other team members can fall into this trap too. For example, Jill and the team put together a harm reduction contract to help her seventy-three-year-old mother that initially involved having Jill make three weekly visits. After about two months, Jill wasn't able to keep this goal. At the next team meeting, her brother convinced Jill to set the more realistic goal of one weekly visit and to hire a home-care nurse for those weeks when Jill needed a break. As Jill's situation illustrates, it's very easy for one or more team members to sway the team into setting unrealistic harm reduction goals.

TIPS FOR GETTING BACK ON TRACK

■ Adopt a slow, baby-step approach at first to build a sense of success and mastery for the entire team.

■ Strive for goals that the person who hoards can't fail at; that is, your loved one will learn something important regardless of outcome.

■ Break down goals into more manageable subgoals. A small but attainable goal is always better than a large one that no one will be able to achieve consistently.

■ Strive for progress, not perfection.

Reason 3: Problems with Rewards

If you notice that your loved one's effort has decreased, discuss with her whether it's time to switch to some other reward that's more meaningful to her. Rewards that are meaningful to, and desired by, your loved one can encourage her to work on her hoarding problem. In addition to being meaningful and desired, rewards must be consistent and accessible, and must closely follow in time the behavior that earned them. By "consistent reward," we mean a reward that you give your loved one every time—without exception and in the same way—she honors her part of the harm reduction contract. It's important for people to receive the rewards they anticipated when they're working on changing behaviors. We recommend that you only agree to rewards that you believe you'll be able to give consistently or sustain. Not only will this help bolster your loved one's motivation, but it also sends the message that you're true to your word.

Rewards work best when they're accessible. An accessible reward is a reward that your loved one can obtain. However, any number of factors can get in the way of your loved one's accessing a reward. You or your loved one may not have the money to go out to dinner, even if that's something that's highly rewarding for him. If your loved one is depressed, it may be difficult to find something that he enjoys doing, or he may be too old and frail to engage in activities that were once pleasurable.

Finally, the closer in time the rewards are to the desired behavior, the more likely the person is to work toward them. It'll be much harder for your loved one to stay motivated if she won't receive reinforcement until months after she has achieved a goal. With the team's help, plan a system whereby you reward your loved one very soon after she reaches any goal.

TIPS FOR GETTING BACK ON TRACK

■ Find out what motivates your loved one and what his specific goals are. These are the rewards to focus on.

■ Access to rewards may be limited due to isolation, physical limitations, or economic status. Select rewards that are accessible, or troubleshoot ways to make them so.

■ Establish rewards that are meaningful, desired, consistent, and that the team can apply relatively close in time to completion of your loved one's target behaviors.

■ Whenever possible, avoid using possessions or granting your loved one's wish to be left alone as rewards.

Reason 4: Other Mental Health Conditions Get in the Way

Mental health problems can hinder the ability of people who hoard to honor their harm reduction contracts, even if they have good insight into the problematic nature of the hoarding behaviors and are highly motivated to work on them.

For example, many people who hoard have trouble staying focused when working on the hoarding problem. Attention deficit/hyperactivity disorder (ADHD) is an inability to attend to a given task for any prolonged amount of time, as well as difficulty following through with tasks that require sustained mental effort. Dottie, for example, had both ADHD and hoarding behaviors. Over the years, Dottie had stored small furniture, boxes, and plastic containers in closets and empty offices at work. She now feared losing her job because of her supervisor's warnings about her hoarding. When Dottie entered the storage areas alone to sort through her possessions, she explained that she felt paralyzed. She would enter the closet, work for a few minutes, and then drift out of the closet for a sip of water. From there, she drifted over to her desk and quickly e-mailed her sister. Dottie was motivated to work on the problem, but her ADHD symptoms made the task much more difficult for her to do on her own. When her harm reduction team revised Dottie's harm reduction plan, they carefully considered Dottie's attention problems to devise strategies to keep her on track.

Depression is another factor that may make it difficult for your loved one to honor his harm reduction contract for several reasons. The first reason is anhedonia, which refers to a loss of pleasure or enjoyment in most things. Take, for example, Cindy, a married and successful accountant who slept on top of a heap of papers on her side of the bed every night. When Cindy started working on the clutter, her husband tried to coax her into meeting her harm reduction goals by offering her what used to be her all-time favorite reward: a night out in the city. However, because Cindy was depressed, she declined and said, "I just don't feel like it. You go ahead. I know I won't have a good time." In addition, when the harm reduction team brainstormed with Cindy about things she might enjoy doing, she couldn't think of anything. If your loved one has dementia, you might see an extreme version of this. Your loved one may voice apathy and show no interest in any pleasurable activity. In Cindy's case, the harm reduction team recommended that she consult a professional to prescribe medication for her depression. Once on medication, Cindy's mood greatly improved, and she began to work steadily on her hoarding problem.

Similarly, if your loved one suffers with post-traumatic stress disorder (PTSD), he may have trouble honoring his harm reduction contract. Shelby was sixty-five years old and had always had a clutter problem. She and her husband had managed the problem over the years, but it had mushroomed after a man broke into their home and robbed them. Although the man didn't harm anyone, Shelby experienced weekly nightmares after the break-in and built a fortress of clutter (papers, boxes, and other items) around her bed to make it difficult for an intruder to reach them. In addition, she created a trail of paper clutter from the front door to the bedroom. She reasoned that the crinkling "clutter alarm" would alert them that someone was in the house. Shelby balked when the team proposed clearing the path of clutter to the door because it made it difficult to exit in an emergency. Shelby and her team brainstormed, and Shelby agreed to install a security system in the home to replace the clutter alarms. Once the team solved this problem, Shelby was more willing to work on her hoarding problem.

TIPS FOR GETTING BACK ON TRACK

- Encourage your loved one to seek medication or cognitive behavioral therapy to address other mental health conditions, such as depression, PTSD, or ADHD, that may be impeding harm reduction work.

- If your loved one isn't open to seeking treatment for mental health issues that interfere with harm reduction, seek solutions with the team about how to work around these complications. For example, people with ADHD might need phone calls during their clearing efforts to keep them on task. People with PTSD might need alternative accommodations to help them feel safe in their homes. People who are depressed might benefit from more frequent social visits to improve their moods and decrease their tendency to withdraw from friends and family members.

Reason 5: Members of the Harm Reduction Team Are Overinvolved

We know that you're desperate to help your loved one. You volunteer to organize and sort his possessions. You're surprised when he says no. You feel an intense urge to go over and throw a few things out for him. You're flabbergasted when he blows up at you and tells you to mind your own business. Alternatively, you're frustrated, hopeless, and frightened, and think, "This is ridiculous. It's taken him three years to clean one room. I can clean the whole house in one week." You take over. We've heard many stories like this. A family member, either well meaning or not, steps in and clears out the loved one's home.

Many times, family members and other team members reason that it's easier and faster to clear the target areas themselves. You might think, "Hey, what's the problem? At least that's an improvement over what's happening now, which is nothing." We agree that sometimes getting your loved one to permit you to clear the target areas and keep them clear is the best you can do. However, there are disadvantages to permitting your loved one to back entirely out of managing her harm reduction plan.

Consider Ellen and Sal, for example. They had been married for forty years when they came to us at their daughter's urging. Although Ellen had agreed to keep papers, books, and boxes off the staircases as part of the harm reduction contract, Sal was the one who usually moved the clutter out of the way. He explained that as long as Ellen did 25 percent of the work, he wanted to chip in and do the other 75 percent because it was easier for him. However, over time, Ellen began pitching in only about 15 percent, then 10 percent, and then hardly at all.

In this situation, Sal was teaching Ellen that if she failed to uphold the contract, he would do it. As you might imagine, this is a slippery slope. First, Ellen stopped clearing the stairs because she knew that Sal would do it. Then she stopped clearing other areas because she knew that Sal would do it. Sal did do it at first, but then grew resentful and soon went on strike, placing him and Ellen at risk.

Ellen and Sal's situation is only one example of how family members become overinvolved in their loved one's harm reduction contract. There are many others. For example, at times, a harm reduction team member takes on the role of the "contract police." He insists that all team members follow every aspect of the harm reduction contract. He harangues them, cajoles them, and even threatens them into following the contract. Over time, this kind of overinvolvement erodes and damages the foundation of any contract: the good will and trust of those who've signed it.

TIPS FOR GETTING BACK ON TRACK

- If you notice yourself erring on the side of overinvolvement in the contract, suggest that another team member pick up part of your role to balance involvement.

- Stick to the agreements in the harm reduction contract. Going above and beyond what the contract designates could be a breech of contract, and the person who hoards could experience this as an affront.

- Apologize to your loved one if you've thrown his possessions away or rearranged his belongings without explicit permission. You can do this in private or in a team meeting. Apologizing in a team meeting has the benefit of having other individuals there who can serve as facilitators and mediators, since the road to forgiveness can be a long and bumpy one.

Reason 6: Lack of Monitoring

An effective harm reduction contract always includes an agreement from your loved one that designated team members may enter her home to monitor her progress (see chapter 6). However, at times, in spite of your best efforts, the harm reduction contract will fail because you didn't get, or because you *lost* over time, an effective way to monitor the hoarding problem.

At times, your loved one will simply bar the door so that you can't get into the home. At other times, access gradually slips away, without fanfare or warning. In addition, access tends to mirror your loved one's motivation. The more open and motivated he is to work on the problem, the more open the door to his home. The less motivated he is, the more likely he is to close the door. You can expect to have many conversations with your loved one about ongoing access to his home. However, while we encourage negotiation, you can't back down when it comes to access. Your primary goal is to get that back. Many times, when you lose access, it means that you haven't done enough of the early work. Go back to chapters 3 and 4 and start there.

At times, you won't be able to monitor a portion of the home because your loved one has blocked the area with clutter. Often this is because your loved one is trying to keep the harm reduction targets in one area clear and doesn't have any other place to put things. If this is the case, designate the paths to these areas as harm reduction targets.

TIPS FOR GETTING BACK ON TRACK

- An unmonitored hoarding problem knows no bounds. Make it a priority to set up routine monitoring of your loved one's home.

- Rotate home visits among team members to avoid overburdening one team member.

- Ask your loved one to send photos of harm reduction targets to increase the rate of monitoring when a home visit isn't possible. Set up the camera to stamp a time and date on each photo so that you can track and verify progress.

- Use glow tape or other visible markers to identify harm reduction targets. This provides a visual reminder that a specific area of the home needs to be a clutter-free zone.

Working Through Contract Failures

The nature of harm reduction contracts is that they fail several times for any number of reasons. Even when contracts fail, the harm reduction process still succeeds as long as members agree to regroup, identify and learn from the reasons the contract failed, and then draft a new contract and try again.

We can't emphasize enough the value of successfully working through contract failures. Working through contract failures provides you and your loved one with opportunities to solve problems in a respectful and collaborative way. When you successfully renegotiate the harm reduction contract, you affirm the goals of harm reduction while strengthening the working relationships between you and your loved one. Listening to, validating, and negotiating with your loved one over many weeks, months, and years will do much to repair the resentment and mistrust you and your loved one have developed over time.

Keeping the Team Together

You can expect, under the best of circumstances, that helping your loved one manage her hoarding problem will be a long and bumpy ride. Over time, you may find yourself growing more jaded or rigid. You may come to meetings determined to make people see it your way and feel less open to the opinions of other team members. This kind of rigidity can block creative problem solving and create more conflict and resentment. Instead, we recommend approaching every team meeting as if it were the first. At first meetings, team members tend to be more calm, patient, and playful. They're less set in their ways and tend to see the problem with fresh eyes.

To set the right tone, you might start team meetings with a brief relaxation exercise. Just a few minutes of breathing slowly or more deeply from the diaphragm can lower the stress temperature of the group. If relaxation exercises aren't your thing, try starting each meeting with a bit of chitchat. Our best team meetings have a "Sunday gathering" tone that includes coffee, snacks, and informal chitchat at the beginning and end of the meeting. A few minutes of chatting can help team members see that they have more in common with the person who hoards than they thought. In addition, after perhaps years of isolation, your loved one is likely starving for some form of normal social interaction.

In addition, try doing something to center yourself before you arrive at the team meetings. If you meditate, jog, or practice yoga, try to do that before the team meeting and encourage others to do the same. If you come to the meeting stressed and pressed for time, your mood will probably affect the other team members, as well as your own satisfaction and effectiveness in the meeting.

Avoiding Contract Burnout

One family member likened the task of managing his mother's hoarding problem to that of Sisyphus, a character from Greek mythology. Zeus punished Sisyphus for his treachery in a particularly agonizing way. For all eternity, Sisyphus rolled a huge boulder up a steep hill, and each time the rock rolled back down again before he reached the top. Although the Greek myth didn't say so, we believe that Sisyphus was a good candidate for burnout.

Burnout is the experience of long-term exhaustion and diminished interest in a task. There'll be times when you or your loved one will feel like Sisyphus. Burnout is normal and can happen to anyone, regardless of how determined, strong, or capable she is. One of the first signs of contract burnout is that you, your loved one, or other harm reduction team members are having trouble maintaining the contract because of feelings of frustration, fatigue, or demoralization. You hear yourself or other team members say that your loved one isn't working as hard as she should. You continue to work but with less effort. You take on fewer tasks and speak up less often. After a while, you simply throw up your hands and give up; this is burnout.

TIPS FOR PROTECTING YOURSELF AND YOUR LOVED ONE FROM CONTRACT BURNOUT

- Directly discuss the issue of burnout at every team meeting. Encourage each team member to discuss why he feels burned out and what, if anything, the team can do to help.

- Protect your loved one from harm reduction burnout by giving her control and independence in the harm reduction process. Small gestures such as asking for permission to visit on a certain day, rather than just assuming that you can come by anytime, reflects the reality that your loved one is an independent person. Whenever possible, ask the person who hoards to choose how she wants things to proceed rather than taking the liberty of moving forward according to your plans or wishes.

- Protect yourself from harm reduction burnout. Take good care of yourself. Eat well, sleep enough, and exercise. This puts you in the strongest position to contribute to the team.

Using Appropriate Pressure

Sometimes family members find that repeatedly reworking the contract after failures isn't enough. Your loved one may want to back out of the harm reduction agreement and may no longer want to keep the harm reduction targets clear. She may find new reasons each month why she can't meet with you to review the home and the contract. In situations where you feel as if you and your loved one have come to a standstill, we recommend proceeding carefully and according to the following guidelines.

First, go back and work on the relationship. This means that you may have to go back and reset the stage for harm reduction (chapter 3) or use L.E.A.P. (chapter 4) to get your loved one back on track. Take your time (if you have it) and be patient. If it worked the first time, it may work again.

Second, if your loved one remains stalled, remind him of the consequences spelled out in his harm reduction contract. Use L.E.A.P. during these discussions and don't threaten him. Third, if your loved one still refuses to accept your help, consider more team meetings during which the designated "bad guy" can apply appropriate pressure. This could be the fire inspector, property manager, or adult protective services worker who's there to remind your loved one that she faces serious consequences if the living situation remains unsafe. This may be the time for the "bad guy" to call regularly or visit your loved one and impress on her the importance of working together to keep the target areas clear.

Last, at times, in spite of your and other harm reduction team members' best efforts, your loved one will change his mind and close the door to further help. If you've run out of time and the authorities tell you that they must step in and take over, read chapter 10 for information on clear-out interventions and how to manage the impact on you and your loved one.

Making a Private Situation Public

In this section, we describe the benefits and risks of the most serious form of appropriate pressure: making a private situation public. A public situation means that authorities know about the hoarding problem. The authorities can include a visiting nurse, an adult protective services worker, a code enforcement officer, or a mental health worker.

We don't take this topic lightly. It's a serious decision with serious implications for you and your loved one. However, this is an essential issue to consider, because it's likely that sooner or later your loved one's situation will become public, whether you do anything or not. Besides, your loved one may be in such great danger that to do nothing is unbearable. In addition to describing the risks and benefits of making a private situation public, we'll describe how to go public if that's what you decide to do. Also, if your loved one's hoarding situation is already public, we describe how you can use this situation to help your loved one manage her hoarding problem over time.

RISKS TO KEEPING A PRIVATE SITUATION PRIVATE

The primary risk of keeping a hoarding situation private is that some harm may befall your loved one as long as he continues to live in the hoarding situation. The assessment of harm potential that you completed in chapter 5 will help you sort through this. A second possible risk of choosing to keep a hoarding situation private is that you miss a source of appropriate pressure. Once a private situation becomes public, whether or not you made the decision, you may be able to use the situation to help your loved one.

RISKS TO MAKING A PRIVATE SITUATION PUBLIC

There are many serious risks to making a private hoarding situation public. The risks are largely personal and financial, but there are emotional risks as well.

Damaged relationships: The decision to make a private hoarding situation public may forever damage your relationship with your loved one. You can expect your loved one to feel betrayed, angry, and deeply hurt. He may then refuse to see you or speak to you or any other family member again. It may damage your relationship with other family members who have different opinions about your loved one's hoarding situation.

Jason experienced this risk firsthand. He told us that he and his sister no longer spoke because of their intense arguments about whether to make their mom's hoarding situation public. "I wanted to tell someone so we could get my mom some help. I thought that if we told someone, this would shake her up enough so that she would at least let us help her. My sister wasn't ready for that. She thought it would destroy my mom. We argued and said some terrible things to each other. As a result, I haven't seen or heard from my sister in over three years."

Lost living situation: Many family members hope that by making a private hoarding situation public, authorities will remove the loved one and clean and repair the home so that the loved one can continue living there. That's not always the case. At times, the residence would no longer be habitable even if the authorities cleaned it. Years of wet or rotting newspapers can damage floorboards or weaken walls, making it unsafe for your loved one to live in her home. For most older adults, the house is the primary financial asset. What will become of your loved one if authorities decide to destroy that asset? Also, consider where your loved one will go if she can't return home. Will she live with you or another family member? Who'll take her in? Can you afford to pay for an alternative living situation, such as an apartment or nursing home?

In addition to potential financial costs to you and your loved one, there are emotional costs of making a private hoarding situation public. The largest is the stress your loved one will experience if he's removed from his home. Under the best of circumstances, moving to a new living situation is a difficult transition. This is particularly true for an older adult who may have lived in his home for thirty, forty, or even fifty years. Older adults typically may have experienced substantial losses as they've aged. Friends and family members may have died. They may have lost the ability to do things they once enjoyed and did easily. They may have lost the ability to care for others and now find that others are taking care of them. In making a private hoarding situation public, your loved one risks yet another loss: the loss of his home. However, home isn't just four walls and a roof. Home can be the comfort of many things: memories, neighbors, and possessions that are so special to your loved one.

Less control of the process: Once a hoarding situation becomes public, believe it or not, you may discover that you have even less control of the situation than before. In our experience, most of the professionals who become involved in a public hoarding situation care about your loved one, but many times they're quite limited in terms of what they can or can't do. The bottom line is that once you make a private hoarding situation public, you may have less say in what happens to your loved one and to the home.

Brenda has experienced this firsthand: "Once authorities discovered my father's hoarding problem, I felt as if all of us were on a fast-moving train that we weren't driving. The fire chief and the code enforcement officers were all telling us, 'I'm sorry, but my hands are tied. This is what has to happen.' I never felt more out of control in my life. I can only imagine how my father felt."

Shame and embarrassment: A final risk is that you and your loved one will likely feel embarrassed or ashamed if the hoarding situation comes to light. How will you feel when you see your father's name in the local newspaper? How will you feel when friends, neighbors, and other family members start asking you about the hoarding problem, or when public officials clear out the premises and cart away all of your loved one's belongings while curious neighbors observe?

Clearly, this is a risky decision for you and your loved one. Again, we urge you not to tell your loved one that you're considering going public unless you're fully prepared to do it. You may want to bring in a mental health professional to sort out the risks and benefits and to facilitate discussions among your family members. However, be aware that if the mental health professional believes that your loved one is in danger, she may have to report the situation and thereby make it public.

BECKY'S CALCULATION OF THE RISKS
AND BENEFITS OF GOING PUBLIC

Keeping the Situation Private	
Risks	**Benefits**
Dad may get hurt in a fire or fall and break his hip.	Spares Dad and the family from the shame and humiliation of others knowing about this.
	We don't have to deal with finding another place for Dad to live if he can't go home.
	Dad is old, and we could enjoy our time together with him rather than destroy what relationship we have with him.
Going Public	
Risks	**Benefits**
Dad will feel betrayed and never speak to us again.	We've tried everything else. Maybe this would force him to accept help.
The problem might get worse if they put him back in his house.	
I don't know where we would put Dad if they remove him from his home. He can't live with me, and Bobbie won't take him in. We can't afford a nursing home.	
Dad has lived in his house for fifty years. He's not well, and this could destroy him.	

Calculating the Risks and Benefits of Going Public

On a piece of paper or in a notebook, list the risks and benefits of making your loved one's hoarding situation public. You can look at Becky's worksheet to get a better idea of how to sort out these issues. We've identified most of the typical risks and benefits, but you may have some that are unique to your and your loved one's situation. Include other family members in the decision-making process, because this is too big of a decision for one person to make alone. The more information and viewpoints you have, the more confident you'll feel about the decision you make. It's essential that all family members agree with the decision, whatever it is, because the entire family will suffer the consequences of what you decide.

Making the Best of a Public Situation

Many times, family members don't decide whether to make their loved one's hoarding problem public. Others make that decision for them. Once this happens, your job is to make the best of a tough situation by using the situation to benefit your loved one now and in the future.

Work with the Authorities

The way we look at it, when a hoarding problem becomes public, there really are no "bad guys." We've spoken to many professionals who are heartbroken when they must force someone to leave her home. They tell us that this is the worst part of their job. Your loved one may tell you that the authorities are forcing her out of her home. However, if anything, the law is what forces your loved one out of her home. The authorities, unfortunately, are there to carry it out.

Once a hoarding problem becomes public, it doesn't do you or your loved one any good to take it out on the authorities. Making the best of the situation means working with the authorities so that they can do what they must in the most caring and compassionate way possible. They can be terrific allies as you try to help your loved one.

Provide Your Loved One with Emotional Support

Once a private hoarding situation becomes public, your loved one will need additional emotional support from you and his community. Once the situation becomes public, your loved one will likely feel humiliated, anxious, and resentful. More people are likely coming into his home, with or without permission. More people are likely insisting that he get help or demanding that he do something immediately to solve the problem. This is the time to reconnect with your loved one.

In addition, you can take the lead in connecting your loved one to resources, such as her church, clubs, or other community organizations. You can ask the authorities for ideas of other support services in your community that can help your loved one.

In this chapter, you learned that there are many reasons why harm reduction contracts veer off track now and again. At those times, we encourage you to take a deep breath and remember that bumps are part of the harm reduction process. If repeated renegotiations fall short of keeping the work progressing, you may be in a situation to consider applying appropriate pressure. The following chapter describes special situations that can make managing a hoarding problem even more difficult, such as when more than one person who hoards lives together or when your loved one with a hoarding problem is frail or suffers with dementia.

CHAPTER 9

All in the Family and Other Complications

As you no doubt know, dealing with hoarding behaviors is tricky. Further complications arise from the fact that hoarding behaviors accompany many different types of mental illnesses. This is especially important in older adults, for whom dementia might be a risk factor. This chapter presents the difficulties that arise in special populations, including older adults, people in assisted-care facilities, and people who hoard who live together in the same residence. With each of these populations, there are unique and specific risks to consider when developing a harm reduction plan. We offer some strategies and solutions to help you navigate through these hurdles.

When People Who Hoard Live Together

If multiple members of a household have hoarding problems, clutter builds up at an exponentially faster rate than if only one person who hoards lived in the home. In addition, people living and hoarding together can battle over turf, jealously protecting certain areas of the home and reserving them for their possessions only. They might argue over space and be resentful if their spaces are the ones most often targeted in the harm reduction contract. They can argue about who discards what or how much. They may even steal from each other.

How does having more than one person who hoards in a residence affect the harm reduction approach? First, it's important that you include all people who contribute to the hoarding problem on the harm reduction team. You can consider the two or more people who hoard as the team *within* the team. This way, each person who contributes to the hoarding problem can be in a position to share responsibility for reducing risk and upholding the contract. Family and team members work together to solve problems about how to ensure and balance that shared responsibility. This is important because failure to maintain the harm reduction contract may result in the same consequence for both (in some cases eviction). As a team, it's therefore useful to underscore the link between the shared responsibility and shared outcomes.

Second, when two or more people who hoard live together, we recommend that you include in the harm reduction contract an explicit agreement about how to manage conflicts about space ("turf wars"). When more than one person who hoards live together, it's essential that you include as a harm reduction goal how they'll share space fairly. Solutions may include designating zones for each person's possessions and making explicit agreements among household members to discard an equal volume of possessions. For example, an agreement that worked for one couple was for the husband to sell ten of his large tools if his wife sorted through and consolidated the contents of ten of her boxes.

When People Who Hoard Live in Assisted-Care Facilities

Family members often worry that an assisted-care facility will either discharge or refuse to take the person who hoards because of her hoarding and cluttering tendencies. However, these types of facilities often work very effectively with people who clutter. Below are some innovative strategies that assisted-care facilities have used to respond to hoarding behaviors. Familiarizing yourself with these can put you in a better position to seek solutions with the staff of your loved one's treatment facility.

Harm Reduction Strategy 1: Provide pleasurable activities outside the person's room. An important harm reduction strategy for people in assisted-care facilities is to reduce isolation by creating rewarding activities that are social and get the person out of his room. Encouraging people to spend more time in a wide range of pleasurable activities that reduce isolation can decrease the amount of time otherwise focused on hoarding and cluttering.

For people who spend much of their time sitting in one chair or lying in bed, bedsores can be a hazard. Bedsores are wounds in the skin that result from prolonged contact and pressure of skin against a surface. Open wounds then create the possibility of infection. Given this risk and others, keeping your loved one up and active has many potential positive effects.

Given your history with your loved one, you probably know better than anyone else what kinds of activities she enjoys. You may know her hobbies, her favorite TV shows, her favorite foods, and the many other details that make her unique. Call on this knowledge to initiate, and suggest to staff to offer, fun and interesting things for your loved one to do. For example, if your loved one likes cooking and fine food, you could suggest starting a "foodie" recreation group at the residence that includes watching a recipe show on TV, trading recipes, or reviewing the food section of the local newspaper.

Harm Reduction Strategy 2: Transfer hoarding of unsafe objects to safe ones. Another important harm reduction strategy is to replace potentially harmful items with safer ones. In the nursing home, Mary, a seventy-eight-year-old widowed mother of three with suspected Alzheimer's disease, kept her soiled undergarments in the top drawer of her bureau. When a nursing home staff worker attempted to remove these garments from the drawer, Mary grabbed on to the garments and literally engaged in a tug-of-war with the nurse. The nurse agreed to trade a greater number of identical clean undergarments for the soiled ones, saying to Mary, "I'll give you these ten clean underpants for those three messy ones." On most days, Mary was amenable to this. On days when she wasn't, Mary instructed the nurse to leave her room. The nurse then came back an hour later to try again. If Mary still refused to trade, the nurse called in another staff worker to remove the soiled garments and replace them with new ones while Mary slept. The nurse explained that she didn't want Mary to distrust her because she spent the bulk of each waking day attending to Mary; she thought it was better to have another nurse potentially be the target of Mary's distrust or aggression in order to maintain their positive relationship. This seemed to work well to reduce harm and maintain a strong alliance.

Another way to promote the exchange of safe items for unsafe ones is to equip a daily "swap cart" with pieces of chewing gum, tea bags, small towels, candies, pens, and other miscellaneous items. Whenever the swap cart visited Mary, the staff member encouraged her to trade her soiled laundry for items on the cart. For several months, Mary was amenable to this strategy. As her dementia progressed, however, Mary disengaged completely from others, including the staff, which forced her care providers to remove her soiled items without negotiation.

Reducing the risk associated with potentially harmful possessions is very important for people with dementia or another condition that might spur aggressive or impulsive behavior. When a person hoards unsafe objects such as silverware, "sharps" (needles taken from the ward), garbage, waste products, or spoiled food, ask him to trade these items for safe items that he may find desirable. If your loved one doesn't have cognitive impairment, you may still need to consider whether hoarded items could contribute to risk of infection. If your loved one is depressed, consider whether he's holding on to things that could facilitate self-harming behaviors. For example, holding on to a plethora of old prescription pills isn't a good idea for anyone and is especially a bad idea for someone with suicidal inclinations.

Harm Reduction Strategy 3: Make changes to the environment. Ever since Elsa moved into the nursing home unit, staff had to remove the medical and desk supplies from her room on a daily basis. Elsa was eighty-two and had collected miscellaneous possessions all her life. The nurses classified Elsa as a "raider," meaning that she found her way into supply spaces and other people's rooms and took whatever pleased her. Elsa usually brought eight or nine small fruit-jam packets back to her room from the breakfast area every morning. Nurses also found gauze, disposable bandages, latex gloves, pens, notepads, and magazines from the common areas in Elsa's closet.

Elsa's situation highlights the importance of intervening directly on an environmental level. As a family member, you can work with staff to seek ways to limit your loved one's access to possessions that don't belong to him or that he doesn't need. For example, by searching for ways to curtail the raiding behavior, the dining room staff at Elsa's facility began delivering Elsa's toast to her with jam already on it and putting the jam trays behind the cafeteria counter. Staff began locking up spaces that were attractive to someone accustomed to acquiring, such as all supply closets and cabinets on the ward. The staff instructed other residents to keep their doors closed if they weren't in their rooms. These interventions were sufficient to keep Elsa's acquiring to a minimum.

In Elsa's case, staff and family members successfully found ways to keep Elsa's hoarding and hiding in check. Most of us aren't born with great problem-solving skills, however. We have to develop them through practice. For an example of how to solve problems, see the sample worksheet on the next page. Then, on a piece of paper, try out the process with a problem you identified with your loved one's hoarding behavior. This exercise can help strengthen your problem-solving skills and increase your ability to work through the typical problems that arise when working with your loved one to manage his hoarding problem.

Problem-Solving Worksheet

1. Identify the problem that needs solving. Write it below:

    Elsa takes too many fruit jams from the breakfast table and keeps them in her room.

2. Generate as many solutions as possible to this problem. Include every solution you can generate, even if at first blush it seems far-fetched or unfavorable. Don't judge or discount a potential solution. Write them all down here next to the S lines (S1, S2, and so on). Later, you'll see how to write down your evaluations next to the E lines (E1, E2, and so on).

    S1: *Stop bringing jam to her table.*

    E1: *She likes jam though. This would be too punishing.*

    S2: *Bring a flavor of jam she doesn't like.*

    E2: *Same point as above.*

    S3: *Bring one or two jams only.*

    E3: *This might work. It wouldn't be problematic if she brought only a couple of jams back to her room.*

    S4: *Bring a small bowl of jam without a lid instead of individual jam packets.*

    E4: *This might work. However, she might go to other tables and take their jam.*

    S5: *Bring a hundred jams to her table so they won't seem as valuable.*

    E5: *This could work.*

S6: *Bring her toast already prepared with jam and hide the rest.*

E6: *This might work the best. She gets to eat jam, but there's none to take back. It'll require extra effort from the staff, but they'll likely be willing.*

3. Now, it's time to evaluate the ideas you generated. Consider each of the possible solutions you wrote down, one at a time. What would work well with each? What wouldn't work so well? Write down your evaluations next to the E lines (E1, E2, and so on).

4. Which solution is your best option to try? *S6.*

Harm Reduction Strategy 4: Accommodate when possible (and to a point). Recently, we received a call from a nurse manager at a local facility who asked what she could do to encourage a new resident to discard possessions that he'd stockpiled on the floor in the corner of his room. When we asked the nurse manager what options there were other than the floor for locations to keep the resident's possessions, she replied that there weren't any. We then suggested that that was the problem to fix, rather than insist that the resident discard his possessions.

The facility management began offering residents one or two large storage bins that were clear so that the residents could easily view their contents. The staff informed residents that the bins had to remain out of the way so that staff and residents could walk easily and safely through the rooms, and that they would immediately remove any possessions located outside of the bins.

Another example is Barry, a sixty-three-year-old veteran living in the VA nursing home because of severe physical impairments. Barry was in the process of filing disability claims with the VA and with social security. Week after week, the nursing home staff noticed increasingly larger piles of financial papers and medical records strewn around Barry's bed and the floor. Add those to his stash of daily newspapers that he liked to keep, and the paper clutter began posing a significant risk for falls. The staff accommodated Barry's needs in two wonderful ways. First, they found him a bigger room. This was preparation for the second accommodation, which was to move a large desk into his room so that he could put all of his papers on a piece of furniture rather than the floor.

In these examples, a simple physical intervention (the manipulation of space and furniture) provided a viable solution to the harm associated with a clutter problem. If a facility has the resources to actually accommodate cluttering to a point while simultaneously reducing harm potential, the outcome will likely be satisfying to all parties involved.

Harm Reduction Strategy 5: Decide when it's okay not to intervene. Sometimes hoarding behaviors may be inconvenient to others, bothersome, or just plain annoying. However, they may not always pose a risk to the person who hoards or to others. If cluttering behaviors among the elderly or those in assisted-care facilities don't interfere with the person's ability to function adequately or pay bills, or if they don't endanger the person or others, then the situation may not require intervention. In these instances, the best course of action may be to establish a good relationship with the person and follow up periodically in case the situation deteriorates.

When the Person Who Hoards Is an Older Adult

Regardless of whether your loved one lives in an assisted-care facility, a hotel, in her own home, or with you, there are special considerations for keeping her safe as she gets older. As people age, there's more clutter to contend with due to many years of unfettered saving and a lifelong reluctance to discard. At the same time, hoarding behaviors tend to cause more problems with age because of the cognitive and physical declines that sometimes accompany the aging process. Older people who hoard are a population at particular risk, because their physical and cognitive deficits make it all the more difficult and, at times, unsafe to live in their residences. Some of the more common ways that being older poses special considerations are in terms of self-neglect and hygiene issues, dementia, and frailty. We discuss these types of issues next.

How Self-Neglect Influences Harm Reduction

When elderly people who hoard also show self-neglect, the primary goal is to improve and maintain the person's hygiene to protect him from infection or disease. Hygiene issues that typically accompany severe hoarding problems include oral or bodily (or both) malodor related to dirt or infection. In severe cases of self-neglect, people may require dentistry to treat gum and tissue infections, and family members may require nursing assistance to change their loved one's undergarments regularly and maintain his hygiene and health.

How Dementia Influences Harm Reduction

Through its effects on cognition and memory, dementia has a huge impact on several life domains of the elderly person, including self-care and autonomy. As families struggle with how to handle the changes incurred by dementia, such as how to handle taking the car keys away from their loved one for good or how to attend to her daily living needs, families also struggle with their loved one's hoarding and hiding behaviors. When both dementia and hoarding are present, the primary aspects that family members will likely contend with are the unique and challenging nature of the types of possessions saved, dealing with hiding behaviors, and dealing with your loved one's allegations that you stole or hid her possessions.

TYPES OF POSSESSIONS

If you've ever cleared out the home of your loved one who hoards, you probably have stories about the unusual possessions you discovered. If your loved one has dementia in addition to hoarding, your stories of what you found might even be difficult to tell. For example, Carrie tearfully reported how she came across twenty pairs of soiled adult diapers and personal undergarments in her mother's dresser when she was putting away the clean laundry.

As the loved one of someone with dementia or other cognitive impairments, you may have come across bags of urine or feces that your loved one was saving. When someone loses his memory, he might forget how to discriminate between trash and nontrash items, or he might forget how to dispose of items he recognizes as trash (Hogstel 1993). You may have come across expired and moldy food in the refrigerator and cupboards of your loved one's home. Spoiled food is common in the kitchens of people who hoard without dementia as well. However, people with dementia may be at greater risk of actually eating such foods, because they can't recognize that some things are no longer safe to eat. This risk extends to other potentially harmful substances in the house, such as cleaning fluids, plant fertilizers, jewelry cleaners, and lotions. Keep these substances out of reach or remove them altogether.

One important strategy for dealing with your loved one's saving of rotten food or waste products is to go beyond just discarding these items in outdoor trash receptacles. People with dementia may rummage through these receptacles and bring those items back into the house. Remove receptacles such as these completely from the premises.

HIDING BEHAVIORS

Hiding behaviors are common among people with dementia. Hiding is an attempt to safeguard belongings by placing them in "secret places." Often, however, the person with dementia forgets where she placed important possessions. Jan's seventy-five-year-old mother, Rita, started showing signs of cognitive decline about a year before Jan brought her into the university health center for an evaluation. Her mother wasn't driving anymore and therefore requested that Jan take her to the bank every three or four days. Rita continually explained to Jan that she wanted to have cash on her "in case of an emergency," and she withdrew hundreds of dollars at a time. Jan and her sisters had no idea what Rita did with the money. Occasionally, Rita wrongly accused Jan of stealing cash from her, which greatly pained Jan. When Rita entered a nursing home several months later and her daughters cleared out her house, they wondered whether they would come across a large stash of bills but never did. They had no idea what happened to the tens of thousands of dollars that Rita likely withdrew over time and theorized that she might have hidden the cash *too well* somewhere in the house.

To help reduce hiding behaviors, keep locked the attic, basement, and unused closet doors in your loved one's home. Padlocks are helpful here, because they can be unlocked only with a key or combination. Clear out closets and keep few things in them so that you can easily check for any new items that your loved one might place there.

ACCUSATIONS AND MISTRUST

Has your loved one ever accused you of taking something from him? If so, we know how hurtful that can be. However, it's a common occurrence for people with memory problems to accuse others of stealing, misplacing, or throwing away their possessions. These allegations are often devastating (and at times infuriating) to loved ones. You can provide gentle reassurance that you didn't take, relocate, or throw away your loved one's possessions (if that's indeed the case) and approach the person with compassion and understanding.

We recommend that you and other family members quickly grow a thick skin, because such suspiciousness and allegations are an unfortunate and common feature of dementia. Remind yourself that the person with cognitive decline doesn't remember what happened to the possession and doesn't know that she has a memory problem. Family members and providers need to see the behavior for what it is, a symptom associated with cognitive impairment, and avoid taking it personally. This usually takes a lot of practice on behalf of the accused person, who, understandably, may be very hurt and defensive about such allegations. Give yourself time to learn to avoid taking the allegations personally, but try to get there as quickly as you can.

How Frailty Influences Harm Reduction

For some, physical health and stability decline as they advance in age. People lose muscle mass, bone density, and the ability to move as quickly as they once did. They may be undernourished or may engage in far less physical activity than they once did. Since frailty influences the risk of people who hoard and live in highly cluttered residences, it can significantly influence the harm reduction plan's design and implementation.

The first consideration is that frailty increases the risk of falling. So does clutter. So putting those two factors together dramatically increases a person's risk of harm. Specifically, as age increases, the risk of hip fracture increases. If your loved one fractures his hip, he'll be immobilized for a long period of time in order to heal. This, in turn, increases the risk of bedsores, muscle loss, embolism, and additional hip fractures in the future.

In addition to amplifying a person's health and safety risks, frailty can also interfere with the harm reduction process itself. Home visits that require ambulation throughout areas of the home, or sorting or removing possessions, may simply take more time as a person's pace decreases with age or frailty.

Finally, frailty also increases the likelihood that people will injure themselves as they try to declutter their living situations. One frail elderly person who presented to treatment for clutter broke three of his ribs by bending over a large rubber storage bin in order to reach something stored just past it.

To minimize the risk of falls or other accidents due to a cluttered living environment, we recommend the following:

Keep pathways clear. Keep clutter out of the walking paths to the home entrances and between rooms. Make sure there's no clutter on stairwells. Be especially wary of loose pieces of paper on the floor. Pieces of paper have the "banana peel" effect and can cause people to slip and fall backward.

Add railings and physical supports. Stairways should have railings. It might help to have a line of furniture strategically placed next to often-used pathways so that elders can hold on to a stable piece of furniture as they move through high-traffic areas of their homes. Consider introducing your loved one to a walker or another physical support device so that she can walk more steadily.

Keep the home well lit. People trip over things when they can't see them. Therefore, install adequate lighting in the rooms and staircases in your loved one's home and make certain that they're always working. Night-lights that automatically go on at night can help reduce falls in the evening. Routine home visits to ensure that the electricity still works are vital to this recommendation.

Replace slippery floor surfaces. If your loved one has hard wood, linoleum, or tile floors throughout the house, it may be time to add area nonslip carpets. If slippery carpets exist in the bathroom or kitchen, remove those. Add nonslip strips to the bottom of the tub. Pin or tack all area rugs firmly to the floor. Carpet tape can help with this, as can tacks or rubber pads. Nonskid treading on stairs can also reduce the risk of falling.

Beware of slippers. Slippers—the name says it all. If your loved one wears slippers around the house, make sure they have a nonskid sole. However, even slippers with rubber or traction-type bottoms are a poor choice of footwear for frail people if they don't conform completely to the foot and fit securely. If your loved one shuffles at all in her footwear, then the footwear could increase her likelihood of falling.

Limit the use of sedatives. Researchers have linked sedatives, especially benzodiazepines (for example, Valium, Xanax, and Ativan), to an increased risk of falls in some elders (Neutel et al. 1996). This is due to the sedative effect of these substances. If your loved one uses benzodiazepines or other sedatives as part of his care, ask him to consider alternative types of treatment for whatever condition the sedatives target. For example, if a frail elder takes benzodiazepines for anxiety, cognitive behavioral interventions or other pharmacological agents might be better treatment alternatives. If your loved one must use sedatives or declines to stop them, encourage him to take them only just prior to going to bed or during other periods when he can be relatively still.

Encourage exercise to build muscle strength. One of the best ways to counteract frailty is to build muscle strength. Your loved one may not agree to discard certain possessions, but she may agree to get up and out for a walk three times a week. Some people who are especially frail may need someone to walk with them to supervise safety.

In this chapter, you learned how managing your loved one's hoarding problem becomes even more difficult if he's frail or lives in an assisted-care facility. In addition, you learned strategies for creating and managing a harm reduction plan when your loved one suffers with dementia or other difficulties because of his age. The final chapter describes some common legal issues that you and your loved one may encounter when working together to manage a hoarding problem, such as when adult or child protective services become involved in the hoarding problem, or when your loved one faces eviction or a clear-out intervention.

CHAPTER 10

When the Landlord Knocks, and Other Terrors

Working on behalf of a loved one with a hoarding problem takes time and effort. It takes patience. It takes many telephone calls and much planning to put together a harm reduction plan and keep it going. Under the best of circumstances this is difficult. However, some of you may face other difficulties in the form of legal issues that threaten to stall your best efforts to help your loved one.

This chapter introduces some of the more common legal issues that you and your loved one may encounter. Please keep in mind that we're psychologists and not legal experts. This chapter is not a substitute for consultation with an attorney or another knowledgeable expert. We encourage you to seek legal consultation when any of the issues described here arises.

There Are No "Bad Guys," Only Potential Team Members

In the face of dealing with legal issues, you may meet many individuals who seem pitted against you or your loved one. The police or fire department may have told your loved one that if she didn't clean her home, they would have to remove her from her home for her own safety. In some cases, municipal officials may not have shown a great deal of patience. It's tempting to view these people as "the bad guys" or "the enemy." However, doing so may not be the best choice if they could help you create and manage a harm reduction plan.

There are many ways to reach out to the "bad guys" and convert them to harm reduction team members. Let's look at how Karen and Miriam did this.

Karen's mother lived in a small studio apartment cluttered with boxes of paper, receipts, plastic bags, and wrapping paper. The property manager, who never yelled but wasn't friendly either, had called her mother weekly to ask what progress she'd made in clearing the apartment. Karen felt that the property manager could be a great ally if she could bring her around to helping her manage her mother's hoarding problem. Karen asked the property manager to lunch to thank her for her patience with the difficult process and to explain that both she and her mother were committed to working on the hoarding problem. At lunch, Karen chatted with the property manager about topics other than her mother. She asked the property manager about her children and what she did for fun. She complemented the property manager's taste in clothing and jewelry. Near the end of the lunch, Karen felt the property manager soften. Karen explained the harm reduction process to her and asked if she would be willing to be a team member. The property manager agreed to think about this. Karen thanked her, and they scheduled another lunch to discuss her mother's progress.

Miriam's story is similar. She had fielded calls from her mother's angry neighbors for years. Her mother hadn't cut the grass in months, the house needed painting, and broken and chipped slate-roof tiles littered the yard. Miriam decided to try to bring some of her mother's neighbors into the harm reduction process. Miriam put a letter in each neighbor's mailbox explaining that her mother had a hoarding problem that made it difficult to maintain her home in the way she would like. She wrote about how much her mother loved the neighborhood and wanted to continue living there for her remaining years. She informed the neighbors that she and her mother were working on the hoarding problem, and asked for their patience.

Having read Karen's and Miriam's stories, think about ways you can reach out to the designated "bad guys" to bring them around to be more tolerant or supportive. The following exercise can help with this.

Converting "Bad Guys" into Team Members

Municipal workers, neighbors, and community members may have legitimate concerns about liability and the rights and well-being of others. Consider the following questions to help yourself see the situation from the other person's perspective. Then, strategize to find ways to bring those individuals over to your loved one's side.

1. Name of person you would like on your side:

    _____

2. Think about the goals or interests of this "bad guy." How do they differ from your or your loved one's goals and interests? List some of this person's goals:

    _____

3. What would be the advantages to having this person on your side?

    _____

4. What information might be helpful for this person to know before taking on a supportive role?

    _____

5. What steps could you take to reach out to this person to change the nature of your relationship? If you're stuck, think back to Karen's and Miriam's efforts to turn adversaries into allies.

    a. _____

    b. _____

    c. _____

TIPS FOR FAMILY MEMBERS

- Reach out to people. Focus on repairing relationships and helping others understand the hoarding problem. Try to empathize with others and find ways to bring them around to working with you.

- Find ways to help people see that there's more to your loved one than the hoarding problem. Encourage your loved one to attend block parties and volunteer at the school to show that he's a caring and responsible community member. You may be surprised at the support you receive.

- Assume the best of people. Many people want to help but may be as confused or frustrated as you've felt over the years. Accept that some people will want to help but others won't.

Adult and Child Protective Services

Adult and child protective services are there to help, although many family members fear what might happen if these professionals discover the hoarding problem and then step in to do their jobs. Family members imagine caseworkers dragging their loved one out of her home kicking and screaming, or removing the children from the home in a storm of sobs and outstretched hands. We hope that never happens, or hasn't happened, to your loved one. However, adult and child protective services workers do have the authority and duty to protect those who they believe aren't able to protect themselves, such as older adults and children, if they believe that they're in danger.

Adult protective services (APS) protect elders (ages sixty-five and older), dependent adults, and people with disabilities. Child protective services (CPS), on the other hand, tend to the safety and well-being of minors, or individuals under eighteen years of age. Although no one (young, middle-aged, or old) is immune from the dangers of living in an extreme hoarding situation, children face particular problems because they're young and may not be able to leave the hoarding situation if they want to. Although many children who live in a hoarding situation cope surprisingly well with the problem, others struggle academically, emotionally, and socially because of the environment in which they live.

If CPS believes that a child is in danger, they ask the family to accept the services they recommend. If the parents refuse to cooperate, they can order the parents to accept the services and remove the children from the home until the parents correct the living situation. Many people who hoard worry that CPS will take their children from them *forever* if they find out about the hoarding problem. That's not the case. If CPS removes children from the home, they then work to reunite the children with the family as soon as it's safe to do so. If possible, they place the children with relatives.

TIPS FOR FAMILY MEMBERS

- Remember that the goal of APS and CPS isn't to divide families. These services work to reunite children with their families once the living situation is safe.

- APS and CPS can provide important resources and people to help manage the hoarding problem. Cooperate with these agencies because they have the same goals that you have for your loved one: to keep everyone who lives in the home safe and comfortable.

- Lessen the negative impact on children living in cluttered environments by taking them to outings, parties, and other social events so that they can socialize with other children. Volunteer your home for birthday parties, children's sleepovers, holiday parties, or other events that your loved one would typically host in his home.

- Encourage your loved one to arrange for her children to be evaluated and possibly to receive psychotherapy or other help. Early intervention can help promote healthy adult development.

Health and Safety Codes

Health and safety codes exist to help us live safely and comfortably in our homes and communities. They also serve as a benchmark for conditions that can initiate legal interventions when a member of the community is out of compliance.

Family members, neighbors, property owners, coworkers, business patrons, or service personnel (such as mail carriers and electric company workers) may call authorities when they happen to catch a glimpse inside the home or become alarmed by the conditions outside the home. The following table lists typical codes violated by those with a significant hoarding problem, although states (and many counties) all have different codes.

COMMON FIRE AND HEALTH CODE VIOLATIONS IN SEVERELY CLUTTERED LIVING ENVIRONMENTS

Fire Code Violations	Health and Safety Code Violations
Blocked entrances or exits (including doors, windows, and hatches)	Inadequate sanitation ■ lack of lavatory, bathtub, or kitchen sink ■ lack of hot or cold running water to plumbing fixtures ■ lack of adequate heating ■ dampness of habitable rooms ■ infestation of insects, vermin, or rodents ■ lack of adequate garbage storage and removal facilities
Lack of functional smoke alarms	Structural hazards ■ deteriorated or inadequate foundations ■ walls, partitions, or other vertical supports that split, lean, or buckle ■ ceilings, roofs, or supports that sag, split, or buckle

Fire Code Violations	Health and Safety Code Violations
Storage of combustible materials ■ too close to heaters or heating devices ■ too close to the ceiling so that it interferes with sprinkler systems ■ in mechanical or electrical equipment rooms	Weeds, junk, dead organic matter, garbage, offal, rodent shelters, stagnant water, combustible materials, and similar materials that constitute fire, health, or safety hazards
Daisy-chaining of extension cords	

Typically, authorities will warn your loved one that if he doesn't correct the health or safety violations, they'll levy hefty fines until he complies. However, fines seldom work if the individual is frail or disabled and therefore unable to correct the problem. In these situations, social interventions can help. For example, some meals-on-wheels programs will send volunteers to help your loved one clear and clean the living space so that it meets minimal health and safety code requirements.

The neglect of certain health and safety codes for an extended period inevitably leads to the deterioration of the conditions of the home. Public health and public works officials may have no other choice than to condemn a property when the residence is dilapidated and uninhabitable, or when it poses a risk to the safety and health of the community. Floors may sag under the weight of tons of debris. Ceilings and roofs may no longer be sound. Insect and rodent infestations are another reason why officials condemn residences. Anyone living in or around the residence may risk respiratory infections or diseases carried by rodents or insects.

TIPS FOR FAMILY MEMBERS

■ Know the gist of fire and health codes. They're your benchmarks for creating a safe and habitable environment. By being familiar with these codes, you're in a better position to help your loved one target those areas of the home that are noncompliant.

■ Consider the structural integrity of your loved one's home. If you suspect rodent or pet damage to the floors, hire an assessor to come out and evaluate the home.

■ Dampness destroys floors and ceilings. Identify the source of damp areas, repair the problem, and air out wet spaces in the home.

■ Remove your stored possessions from your loved one's home. If authorities condemn your loved one's home because of serious health and safety code violations, they'll board up the home and may remove your possessions along with everything else.

Guardianship or Conservatorship

If you fear that your loved can no longer care for her basic needs or manage her finances, you might consider a *conservatorship* (also called *guardianship* in some areas). A conservatorship allows an individual or agency to make decisions on another's behalf in order to protect her interests. The court appoints conservatorships and typically grants them for one year. They can be renewed or terminated at any time. A conservator can be a family member, friend, public guardian, or private professional (a private agency or professional, such as an attorney, accountant, or clinician). A public guardian typically becomes the conservator by default when there's no willing or qualified loved one, or when the person under the conservatorship can't afford a private conservator.

Once a court appoints a conservator, the conservator determines what arrangements are necessary to provide the person with his basic needs. These include food, clothing, shelter, and medical treatment. Conservatorships can be limited to provide protections over specific domains and not others. For example, conservatorships can focus on ensuring that the person is clothed, fed, and housed, or on protecting the estate, which involves managing money and assets.

When used thoughtfully and with the best interests of your loved one in mind, there are benefits to a conservatorship. A conservatorship can help your loved one live independently in her home longer, thus postponing a move into an assisted-care facility. Public conservatorships can provide a means to increase social support for your loved one, as well as a means to monitor her safety through routine visits to her home.

TIPS FOR FAMILY MEMBERS

- Procedures for a conservatorship vary by state. Learn more about conservatorships by contacting your local department of aging services or adult protective services.

- If you're a conservator for your loved one, seek support and assistance wherever you can find them. If you're the primary caretaker for your loved one, ask family members or friends to step in so that you can have a break from your duties.

Eviction Notices

By the time your loved one receives his first eviction notice, he has likely already received numerous complaints and warnings about the condition of his living situation. If there's the threat of eviction, there are two options to explore simultaneously. You can seek legal help to keep your loved one in his home, and you can work with the property manager and invite him or her to join the harm reduction team.

Seek Legal Help

If the property manager has served your loved one an eviction notice, immediately contact an eviction defense lawyer or volunteer legal representative. Depending on the parameters of the case, eviction defense attorneys may be able to contest the eviction in court. Legal experts often call these types of cases "unlawful detainer cases."

Unlawful detainer cases boil down to four relatively straightforward questions: (1) Did the tenant commit a nuisance? (2) Does the defendant suffer from a disability? (3) Did the tenant request a reasonable accommodation pertaining to the disability? and (4) Did the property owner offer the tenant a reasonable accommodation for that disability?

Nuisance: A nuisance exists if there's a health and safety code violation or if there's a threat or serious inconvenience caused by the clutter in the property. In the least arbitrary of conditions, the fire or building inspector may present an opinion about whether the tenant's housing condition represents a nuisance.

Disability: The court is looking for evidence of a diagnosable medical or mental health illness that caused the alleged nuisance. Thus, your loved one will need written documentation from a diagnostic evaluation by a qualified mental health professional.

Reasonable accommodation: This inquiry concerns whether the tenant requested a reasonable accommodation and, if the tenant made such a request, whether the property owner or manager offered your loved one a reasonable accommodation for her disability. Reasonable accommodations for situations that involve hoarding include time extensions in order to make changes that address the original nuisance and application of behavioral treatments and medications to address the problem. If the answer is no, your loved one may be able to file suit against the property owner for violation of the Fair Housing Act, which prohibits discrimination against individuals suffering from a physical or mental impairment that substantially impairs the ability to perform a major life activity.

Contact the Property Manager

In addition to seeking legal representation, you may want to contact the property owner directly to negotiate and invite the person onto the harm reduction team. You'll want to ask the specific reason for the eviction notice, because eviction notices don't always specify the reason for eviction. Consider Greg, for example, who told his daughter, Julie, that the property owner was threatening to evict him because of clutter that was building up throughout the apartment. Upon speaking with the property owner, however, Julie found out that the eviction notice was in response to three months of bounced rent checks on her father's behalf. Greg was unaware of the problem with his rent checks because he hadn't opened his mail in several months.

By the time your loved one receives an eviction notice, there may have been numerous verbal or written warnings. Therefore, the property owner may legitimately perceive that she has already demonstrated considerable flexibility and leniency. However, it wouldn't hurt to ask whether you can negotiate an extension. Sometimes, the property owner will be more flexible once she learns that a mental health professional has diagnosed the tenant with a mental health disability that has created the reason for eviction.

TIPS FOR FAMILY MEMBERS

- Don't assume that your loved one is off the landlord's or property manager's radar. Ask your loved one whether he has received any written complaints or telephone calls about the hoarding problem. If your loved one has received an eviction notice, obtain a copy so that you have all the relevant information.

- Property managers may hand-post or mail eviction notices. Therefore, an important harm reduction strategy is for your loved one to open the mail regularly. If this is difficult for her, ask if you can do it for her.

- Get legal help if your loved one is in an eviction case. Your loved one has rights that can forestall eviction.

- Encourage your loved one to receive an evaluation by a mental health professional with expertise in hoarding. It's essential that you and your loved one have at your immediate disposal a report showing a diagnosis and the description of the impairment caused by the clutter. Finding a hoarding expert can be challenging, but contacting resources in the appendix can help.

- If authorities evict your loved one, call your local social services department. The authorities who evicted your loved one will likely have contact information for alternative housing and may have already placed calls.

- Know your loved one's legal rights. For more information about tenant rights in your state, visit www.hud.gov/renting/tenant-rights.cfm online, or call the U.S. Department of Housing and Urban Development at 202-708-1112.

Clear-Out Interventions

In a clear-out intervention, municipal authorities step in and remove the bulk of the possessions from a home in order to protect the health and safety of those who live there. Typically, a clear-out is a last-ditch effort in a series of failed interventions by officials and family members. A single clear-out intervention can cost the town or county tens of thousands of dollars in labor and special equipment or cleaning services. Furthermore, a clear-out does little to change a hoarding problem.

TIPS FOR FAMILY MEMBERS

■ Recognize that a clear-out intervention can be traumatic for your loved one. Ask your loved one what you can do to help. Think about what will make this day easier on you too.

■ Find out and then explain to your loved one who's likely to be present (types of county officials and support personnel) and what their roles are in the clear-out intervention (see the following table).

■ Suggest that your loved one take a limited number of pictures of particularly treasured objects to preserve their memory. This may be a helpful way of retaining a physical connection with a proportion of belongings (Cermele, Melendez-Pallitto, and Pandina 2001).

■ Ask to relocate family heirlooms or photos that you don't want confiscated from your loved one's home to your home. There may not be enough time to find and relocate them once the county has ordered the clear-out intervention.

■ Remember that clear-out interventions create a clean slate for the residence but not the hoarding problem. Give your loved one some time to grieve the losses of the clear-out and then gently encourage her to resume harm reduction work to prevent future clear-outs.

AUTHORITIES LIKELY TO ATTEND
A CLEAR-OUT INTERVENTION

Representative	Role
Social, protective, or mental health services	Assess for diminished capacity (cognitive impairment) and harm to incapacitated adults, and help access resources
Health department	Assesses overall property maintenance compliance and the home's habitability
Building inspector	Assesses structural soundness of the residence and functioning of electricity, plumbing, and sewage
Police	Provide assistance and transportation off the premises, if needed
City attorney	Provides advice on matters of municipal concern
Fire department	Assesses fire code violations
Housing representative	Locates alternative housing, if needed
Animal control worker or the Humane Society	Finds alternative housing and provides on-site medical attention to animals

In this chapter, you learned about the multiple legal issues that can come into play when someone you love has a hoarding problem and about many of the players, such as adult protective services and code enforcement officers. In addition, you've learned about a guardianship or conservatorship as a way to manage the hoarding problem. Finally, you learned how best to handle eviction notices when the hoarding problem comes to the attention of municipalities and how best to work with state and local agencies who've declared their intention to clear out your loved one's home.

Resources

Recommended Reading

Jampolsky, G. G. 1999. *Forgiveness: The Greatest Healer of All.* Hillsboro, OR: Beyond Words Publishing.

Kolberg, J. 2008. *What Every Professional Organizer Needs to Know About Hoarding.* Atlanta, GA: Squall Press.

Kolberg, J., and K. Nadeau. 2002. *ADD-Friendly Ways to Organize Your Life.* New York: Brunner-Routledge.

Landsman, K. J., K. M. Rupertus, and C. Pedrick. 2005. *Loving Someone with OCD: Help for You and Your Family.* Oakland, CA: New Harbinger Publications.

Luskin, F. 2002. *Forgive for Good: A Proven Prescription for Health and Happiness.* New York: HarperCollins Publishers.

————. 2007. *Forgive for Love: The Missing Ingredient for a Healthy and Lasting Relationship.* New York: HarperCollins Publishers.

Neziroglu, F., J. Bubrick, and J. A. Yaryura-Tobias. 2004. *Overcoming Compulsive Hoarding: Why You Save and How You Can Stop.* Oakland, CA: New Harbinger Publications.

Smedes, L. B. 2007. *Forgive and Forget: Healing the Hurts We Don't Deserve* (2nd ed.). New York: HarperCollins Publishers.

Steketee, G., and R. O. Frost. 2007. *Compulsive Hoarding and Acquiring: Workbook.* New York: Oxford University Press.

Tolin, D. F., R. O. Frost, and G. Steketee. 2007. *Buried in Treasures: Help for Compulsive Acquiring, Saving, and Hoarding.* New York: Oxford University Press.

Professionals Who Can Help

Child and Elder Services

Child and elder protective services aim to provide assessment and assistance when needed. These services are usually county based, so you can look up the number for the protective services agency in your specific county.

Cleaning and Hauling Services

There are many types of cleaning services available, from agencies that specialize in hauling away clutter and junk to those that specialize in removing human waste.

Crime scene cleanup agencies also provide assistance in homes of people who hoard. An important consideration, however, is whether you or your loved one would want a truck in the driveway with a crime scene cleanup logo on it. This could be very stigmatizing and unnecessarily painful (A. Merrifield, pers. comm.).

Conservators

Conservators can help incorporate financial protection in the harm reduction plan for your loved one. You can find a private or public conservator by contacting a local social services agency such as adult protective services or through your county government's department of aging, or by asking your family physician for a referral.

The Humane Society

Most local branches of the Humane Society routinely deal with animal hoarding situations. In the best-case scenario, your local chapter has a mobile spay, neuter, and vaccination clinic that can provide curbside services at the residence, because many individuals who hoard animals won't permit the animals to leave the premises. Find out how your local branch of the Humane Society handles animal hoarding situations if this pertains to your loved one's situation.

Legal Advocates

Legal advocates play a central role in hoarding cases that involve eviction, property damage, or discrimination. Many cities and states have volunteer legal services programs that offer free or low-fee assistance. Typing "volunteer legal services" in a search engine brings up many options, and hopefully there'll be a local resource available to you.

Mental Health Providers

Mental health providers can help mediate harm reduction teams. Also, if your loved one becomes interested in treatment for hoarding, psychologists and other providers who have training in cognitive behavioral treatments are likely to be the best qualified.

Psychiatrists have a medical degree and can prescribe medication. You may be able to find qualified psychiatrists through your own personal and professional networks, including your primary care physician.

Social workers are particularly skilled at finding resources for clients. They may be more likely to provide home visits than other clinicians because their intervention model emphasizes the importance of the home environment.

Occupational Therapists

Occupational therapists assess how well someone can perform activities of daily living (such as bathing, eating, and getting dressed), and then find ways to help implement better methods for reaching these ends.

Professional Organizers

Many professional organizers are familiar with ways to help people who hoard. There are several benefits associated with using a professional organizer, including having someone work on-site at your loved one's home who may be more affordable than a mental health professional.

Wildlife Management and Pest Removal Agencies

When there's a rodent or insect infestation, animal wildlife or pest removal agencies are essential members of a harm reduction team. You can call professionals to help fumigate for insects or bait and trap rodents.

Support Groups

Group and Contact Info	Purpose
Alzheimer's Association www.alz.org	Find your local chapter and then click "Support Groups" to find a group in your area; "Lotsa Helping Hands" is a free online tool that assists family members and caregivers in coordinating home visits with one another.
Bay Area Resources: Support Groups www.hoarders.org/sg.html	A website supported by Peninsula Community Services in the San Francisco Bay Area that provides resources and information about support groups in the Bay Area and beyond.
Children of Hoarders www.childrenofhoarders.com	Has an online chat room for family members; also includes a list of interdisciplinary task forces by state.
Clutterers Anonymous www.clutterersanonymous.net 310-281-6064	A self-help 12-step organization with chapters throughout the United States.

Clutterless Recovery Groups, Inc. www.clutterless.org	National organization that provides newsletters, literature, information, referrals, conferences, pen pals, and group meeting locations.
Mental Health Association of San Francisco (MHA-SF) www.mha-sf.org 415-421-2926	Has groups for family members and for individuals who hoard; also offers an annual conference on hoarding and cluttering.
Messies Anonymous www.messies.com	A central site for online support, group information, tips on organizing, and encouraging messages for those with clutter problems.
Obsessive Compulsive Foundation www.ocfoundation.org 617-973-5801	An international nonprofit organization devoted to education about OCD, outreach and support for OCD sufferers, and support for research into obsessive-compulsive phenomenology and treatment.

Other Resources

Academy of Cognitive Therapy
www.academyofct.org
267-350-7683

American Occupational Therapy Association
www.aota.org
301-652-2682

American Psychological Association
www.apa.org
800-374-2721

Anxiety Disorders Association of America
www.adaa.org
240-485-1001

Association of Behavioral and Cognitive Therapies
www.abct.org
212-647-1890

Attention Deficit Disorder Association
www.add.org
800-939-1019

Hoarding of Animals Research Consortium (HARC)
www.tufts.edu/vet/cfa/hoarding/index.html

National Alliance on Mental Illness
www.nami.org
800-950-6264

National Institute of Mental Health
www.nimh.nih.gov
866-615-6464

National Organization of Professional Organizers
www.napo.net
856-380-6828

National Study Group on Chronic Disorganization
www.nsgcd.org
314-416-2236

New York City Hoarding Task Force
www.environmentalgeriatrics.com/home_safety/clutter.html

Tips for Managing Paper, Mail, and E-mail

Stop the marketing madness. To opt out of direct-mail solicitations, contact the Stop Waste Partnership through its website, www.stopjunkmail.org. There's an online Stop Junk Mail Kit that describes how you can reduce junk mail, or you can call 877-STOPWASTE (786-7927).

You can also contact Valassis to request removal from its mailing lists at www.valassis.com or 860-285-6100.

To stop receiving PennySaver or Valpak coupons, use the form at the end of this section.

Stop the catalogs. Sign up at www.catalogchoice.org to decline unwanted catalogs.

Say no to credit card offers. To opt out of solicitations from credit card companies, call 888-567-8688 or visit www.optoutprescreen.com online. However, be prepared to give out some personal information, such as your Social Security number.

Pay bills online. Most utility, credit card, and loan companies provide the option of securely paying your bill online. Check each of your bills to see if there's a website listed where you can look into this option.

Cancel subscriptions. If you routinely receive multiple magazines or newspapers, consider reducing the number of your subscriptions by 50 percent.

Keep important papers separate. No matter how foreign it may seem to your loved one, it's essential that he set up and practice using a filing system for important papers (Tolin, Frost, and Steketee 2007b). You can help your loved one determine the necessary file labels or categories. Your loved one will need to schedule a specific time at least once a week to file papers and keep the system current and orderly.

Stop the spam. Shop around for an Internet service provider (ISP) that screens for and diverts spam (unwanted e-mails from people you don't know) to keep it out of your or your loved one's in-box.

SAMPLE LETTER TO MARKETERS TO REMOVE YOUR ADDRESS FROM MAILING LISTS

(in this case, PennySaver and ValPak)

Date: _____

PennySaver   ValPak
2830 Orbiter St.   8605 Largo Lakes Dr.
Brea, CA 92821   Largo, FL 33773

To Whom It May Concern:

I want to reduce the amount of unsolicited mail I receive. Please remove my name and address, as listed below, from your mailing list.

Name: _____

Address: _____

City: _____ State: _____ Zip: _____

Thank you.

Signature: _____

Where to Donate or Recycle

Goodwill Industries International (www.goodwill.org) accepts donations of clothing, furniture, books, audio equipment, electronics, and even vehicles. Most of their proceeds go directly to funding training and employment programs for individuals in need, so donating possessions to Goodwill is a great deed.

The Salvation Army (www.salvationarmyusa.org) accepts charitable donations, and its proceeds go toward social services.

Earth911.com (www.earth911.org) provides the location of your nearest recycling center and offers information about recycling everything, even used motor oil (many auto shops collect used motor oil and recycle it for you).

EcoHaul (www.ecohaul.com or 1-800-ECOHAUL) can help get your loved one's possessions to a recycling or donation center.

References

Amador, X., with A.-L. Johanson. 2000. *I Am Not Sick, I Don't Need Help! Helping the Seriously Mentally Ill Accept Treatment: A Practical Guide for Families and Therapists*. Peconic, NY: Vida Press.

Cermele, J. A., L. Melendez-Pallitto, and G. J. Pandina. 2001. Intervention in compulsive hoarding. *Behavior Modification* 25 (2):214–32.

Denning, P. 2000. *Practicing Harm Reduction Psychotherapy: An Alternative Approach to Addictions*. New York: The Guilford Press.

Frost, R. O., and R. C. Gross. 1993. The hoarding of possessions. *Behaviour Research and Therapy* 31 (4):367–81.

Frost, R. O., and T. L. Hartl. 1996. A cognitive-behavioral model of compulsive hoarding. *Behaviour Research and Therapy* 34 (4):341–50.

Frost, R. O., and G. Steketee. 1998. Hoarding: Clinical aspects and treatment strategies. In *Obsessive-compulsive disorders: Practical management*, 3rd ed., ed. M. A. Jenike, L. Baer, and W. E. Minichiello, 533–54. St. Louis, MO: Mosby Press.

———. 1999. Issues in the treatment of compulsive hoarding. *Cognitive and Behavioral Practice* 6 (4):397–407.

Frost, R. O., G. Steketee, and L. Williams. 2000. Hoarding: A community health problem. *Health and Social Care in the Community* 8 (4):229–34.

Hogstel, M. O. 1993. Understanding hoarding behaviors in the elderly. *American Journal of Nursing* 93 (7):42–45.

Hwang, J. P., S. J. Tsai, C. H. Yang, K. M. Liu, and J. F. Lirng. 1998. Hoarding behavior in dementia: A preliminary report. *American Journal of Geriatric Psychiatry* 6 (4):285–89.

Kim, H-J., G. Steketee, and R. O. Frost. 2001. Hoarding by elderly people. *Health and Social Work* 26:176–84.

Luskin, F. 2002. *Forgive for Good: A Proven Prescription for Health and Happiness.* New York: HarperCollins Publishers.

Marlatt, G. A. 1996. Harm reduction: Come as you are. *Addictive Behaviors* 21 (6):779–88.

———. 1998. Harm reduction around the world: A brief history. In *Harm reduction: Pragmatic strategies for managing high-risk behaviors,* ed. G. A. Marlatt, 30–48. New York: The Guilford Press.

Marlatt, G. A., and S. F. Tapert. 1993. Harm reduction: Reducing the risks of addictive behaviors. In *Addictive behaviors across the life span: Prevention, treatment, and policy issues,* ed. J. S. Baer, G. A. Marlatt, and R. J. McMahon, 243–73. Newbury Park, CA: Sage Publications.

Neutel, C. I., J. P. Hirdes, C. J. Maxwell, and S. B. Patten. 1996. New evidence on benzodiazepine use and falls: The time factor. *Age and Ageing* 25 (4):273–78.

Neziroglu, F., J. Bubrick, and J. A. Yaryura-Tobias. 2004. *Overcoming Compulsive Hoarding: Why You Save and How You Can Stop.* Oakland, CA: New Harbinger Publications.

Rogers, C. R. 1951. *Client-Centered Therapy: Its Current Practice, Implications, and Theory.* Boston: Houghton-Mifflin.

Samuels, J. F., O. J. Bienvenu, M. A. Grados, B. Cullen, M. A. Riddle, K. Liang, W. W. Eaton, and G. Nestadt. 2008. Prevalence and correlates of hoarding behavior in a community-based sample. *Behaviour Research and Therapy* 46 (7):836–44.

Steketee, G., and R. O. Frost. 2007. *Compulsive Hoarding and Acquiring: Workbook.* New York: Oxford University Press, Inc.

Tolin, D. F., R. O. Frost, and G. Steketee. 2007a. An open trial of cognitive-behavioral therapy for compulsive hoarding. *Behaviour Research and Therapy* 45 (7):1461–70.

———. 2007b. *Buried in Treasures: Help for Compulsive Acquiring, Saving, and Hoarding.* New York: Oxford University Press.

Tolin, D. F., R. O. Frost, G. Steketee, K. D. Gray, and K. E. Fitch. 2008. The economic and social burden of compulsive hoarding. *Psychiatry Research* 160 (2):200–11.

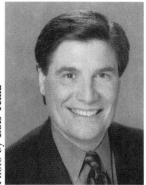

Photo by Lois Tema

Michael A. Tompkins, Ph.D., is a licensed psychologist and a founding partner of the San Francisco Bay Area Center for Cognitive Therapy, an assistant clinical professor at the University of California, Berkeley, and a founding fellow of the Academy of Cognitive Therapy. He has authored and coauthored numerous articles and books on cognitive behavior therapy and related topics, including *My Anxious Mind* and the book and video series *Essential Components of Cognitive-Behavior Therapy for Depression.* He has presented nationally on the topic of compulsive hoarding and is a member of the San Francisco Task Force on Hoarding. He specializes in the treatment of anxiety disorders in adults, adolescents, and children and is in private practice in Oakland, CA.

Tamara L. Hartl, Ph.D., is an independent clinical practitioner in Saratoga, CA, and a psychologist at the VA Palo Alto Health Care System. She has coauthored several seminal publications on hoarding behavior, including the first cognitive-behavioral model for the treatment of compulsive hoarding with Randy Frost. She specializes in the treatment of anxiety disorders and sexual dysfunction as well as compulsive hoarding.

Foreword writer **Randy O. Frost, Ph.D.,** teaches abnormal psychology at Smith College in Northampton, MA. He is coauthor of *Buried in Treasures.*

Foreword writer **Gail Steketee, Ph.D.,** is a professor and co-chair in the department of clinical practice at the School of Social Work at Boston University. She is coauthor of *Buried in Treasures.*

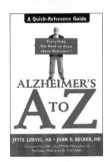
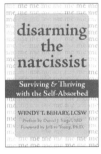
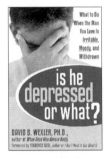